Optimizing Resource Allocation for Small Business Success

How to Allocate Resources Like a Pro: A Guide for Small Businesses

HARRELL HOWARD

Table of Contents

Introduction

We all know that small businesses are facing numerous challenges in today's competitive terrain. One of the most critical factors that can make or break a small business is how effectively it allocates its resources. Resource allocation isn't just about managing money; it encompasses every aspect of a business, from human capital to technology and time management.

This article aims to provide small business owners, managers, and entrepreneurs with a comprehensive guide to optimizing resource allocation. We'll explore why resource allocation is so crucial for small businesses and how it can be the key to unlocking growth, profitability, and long-term success.

Throughout this article, we'll look into various aspects of resource allocation, offering practical insights, strategies, and tools that you can apply to your business immediately. Whether you're just starting out or looking to take your established small business to the next level, the principles and techniques discussed here will help you make the most of your available resources.

By the end of this article, you'll have a deeper understanding of:

- What resource allocation really means and why it's so important
- How to assess and optimize your current resources
- Strategies for effective financial, human, technological, and operational resource management
- Time management techniques to boost productivity
- Methods for monitoring and adjusting your resource allocation strategies

Let's embark on this journey to unlock the full potential of your small business through smart resource allocation.

Chapter 1: Understanding Resource Allocation

What is Resource Allocation?

At its core, resource allocation is the strategic distribution of an organization's available resources across various projects, departments, or activities. It's about making informed decisions on how to use what you have to achieve your business goals most effectively.

Resource allocation isn't a one-time task; it's an ongoing process that requires constant evaluation and adjustment. It involves analyzing your current resources, understanding your business objectives, and finding the best way to align the two.

The key principles of effective resource allocation include:

1. Prioritization: Focusing on the most important tasks and projects that align with your business goals.
2. Efficiency: Maximizing the use of resources to get the best possible outcomes.
3. Flexibility: Being able to adapt and reallocate resources as circumstances change.

4. Balance: Ensuring that all areas of the business receive adequate resources without overcommitting to any single aspect.

Types of Resources

When we talk about resources in a business context, we're referring to a wide range of assets and inputs. Let's break down the main types of resources that small businesses need to manage:

1. **Financial Resources**: This is perhaps the most obvious type of resource. It includes:
   - Cash and liquid assets
   - Credit lines and loans
   - Investments and financial instruments
2. **Human Resources:** Often described as a company's most valuable asset, this includes:
   - Employees and their skills
   - Management expertise
   - External consultants and freelancers
3. **Physical Resources:** These are the tangible assets of your business, such as:
   - Office space or retail locations
   - Equipment and machinery
   - Inventory and supplies

4. **Technological Resources:** In our digital age, these are increasingly important:
   - ○ Hardware (computers, phones, servers)
   - ○ Software and applications
   - ○ Data and information systems
5. **Time as a Resource:** Often overlooked but critically important:
   - ○ Working hours of employees
   - ○ Project timelines
   - ○ Time-to-market for products or services

Each of these resource types plays a crucial role in your business operations, and how you allocate them can significantly impact your success.

Importance of Efficient Resource Allocation

Efficient resource allocation is not just a nice-to-have; it's a necessity for small businesses looking to thrive in competitive markets. Here's why it's so crucial:

1. **Impact on Profitability:**
   Proper resource allocation directly affects your bottom line. By ensuring that resources are used where they'll generate the most value, you can increase efficiency and reduce waste. This leads to lower costs and potentially higher revenues,

ultimately boosting profitability. For example, if you allocate your marketing budget to channels that provide the best return on investment, you're likely to see higher sales without increasing spending.

2. **Enhancing Competitive Advantage:** In a world where small businesses often compete with larger, more resource-rich companies, smart resource allocation can level the playing field. By focusing your limited resources on your core competencies and areas of competitive advantage, you can outperform larger competitors in specific niches. Consider a small tech startup that allocates a significant portion of its budget to research and development. This focus could lead to innovative products that larger, less agile competitors can't match.

3. **Ensuring Sustainability:** Efficient resource allocation is key to long-term sustainability. It helps you avoid common pitfalls like cash flow problems, burnout, or overexpansion. By carefully managing your resources, you can ensure that your business has what it needs to weather economic downturns,

adapt to market changes, and seize new opportunities as they arise.

4. **Improving Decision Making:**
The process of resource allocation forces you to critically examine your business operations and priorities. This leads to better, more informed decision-making across all aspects of your business. When you're clear about where your resources are going and why, you're better equipped to make strategic decisions about growth, product development, hiring, and more.

5. **Enhancing Operational Efficiency:**
Proper resource allocation helps streamline operations by ensuring that each part of your business has what it needs to function optimally - no more, no less. This can lead to improved productivity, faster turnaround times, and better quality products or services.

6. **Facilitating Growth:**
As your business grows, the complexity of managing resources increases. Establishing good resource allocation practices early on creates a scalable framework that can support your business as it expands. This might mean

having systems in place to quickly reallocate resources to new opportunities or having the financial discipline to invest in growth while maintaining operational stability.

7. **Improving Employee Satisfaction and Retention:**
When human resources are allocated effectively, employees are more likely to feel that their skills are being utilized properly and that they have the tools they need to succeed. This can lead to higher job satisfaction and lower turnover rates. For instance, allocating resources for professional development can show employees that you're invested in their growth, increasing their loyalty to your company.

8. **Risk Management:**
Proper resource allocation includes setting aside resources for contingencies. This preparedness can be crucial for managing unexpected challenges or capitalizing on unforeseen opportunities. Having a cash reserve or maintaining flexible staffing arrangements are examples of how resource allocation contributes to risk management.

In the next chapter, we'll look into how you can assess your current resources - the crucial first step in optimizing your resource allocation strategy. Understanding what you have to work with is key to making informed decisions about where and how to allocate your resources for maximum impact.

Chapter 2: Assessing Your Current Resources

Before you can optimize your resource allocation, you need a clear picture of what resources you currently have at your disposal. This chapter will guide you through the process of conducting a comprehensive resource audit and analyzing your findings. Understanding your current resource landscape is crucial for making informed decisions about future allocations and identifying areas for improvement.

The Importance of Resource Assessment

Resource assessment is the foundation of effective resource allocation. It provides a snapshot of your organization's current state, highlighting strengths, weaknesses, and potential areas for optimization. This process allows you to:

1. Identify underutilized or overutilized resources
2. Uncover hidden assets or capabilities
3. Recognize inefficiencies in current allocation practices
4. Establish a baseline for measuring future improvements
5. Align resources with strategic goals

By thoroughly assessing your resources, you set the stage for more informed decision-making and strategic planning.

Conducting a Resource Audit

A resource audit is a systematic review of all the resources available to your business. It's a crucial step in understanding your current position and identifying areas for improvement. Let's break down the audit process for each type of resource:

Financial Audit

A financial audit involves a thorough review of your business's financial health. This includes:

Reviewing Financial Statements

1. **Balance Sheet:** This provides a snapshot of your company's financial position at a specific point in time. It shows:
   - Assets: What the company owns
   - Liabilities: What the company owes
   - Equity: The difference between assets and liabilities

2. **Income Statement:** This shows your company's profitability over a specific period. Key components include:
    - Revenue: Money earned from sales or services
    - Expenses: Costs incurred to generate revenue
    - Net Income: The difference between revenue and expenses
3. **Cash Flow Statement:** This tracks the inflow and outflow of cash in your business. It's divided into:
    - Operating activities
    - Investing activities
    - Financing activities

Analyzing Cash Reserves and Liquidity

Assess your company's ability to meet short-term obligations by looking at:

- Working capital ratio (current assets / current liabilities)
- Quick ratio ((current assets - inventory) / current liabilities)

- Cash ratio (cash and cash equivalents / current liabilities)

Evaluating Outstanding Debts and Credit Lines

Review:

- Long-term debts
- Short-term loans
- Credit lines and their utilization
- Interest rates and repayment terms

Assessing Profitability of Different Products or Services

Conduct a profitability analysis for each product or service line:

- Calculate gross profit margins
- Analyze contribution margins
- Identify high-performing and underperforming offerings

Reviewing Financial Ratios

Key ratios to consider include:

- Profit margins (gross, operating, and net)
- Return on Investment (ROI)

- Return on Assets (ROA)
- Return on Equity (ROE)
- Debt-to-Equity ratio

Tools like QuickBooks or Xero can be helpful in gathering this financial data. Remember, the goal is to get a clear picture of where your money is coming from and where it's going.

Human Resource Audit

This involves taking stock of your workforce and their capabilities:

List All Employees, Their Roles, and Responsibilities

Create a comprehensive employee database including:

- Name and position
- Department or team
- Key responsibilities
- Reporting structure

Assess Skills and Competencies Within Your Team

Conduct a skills inventory:

- Technical skills
- Soft skills
- Certifications and qualifications
- Experience levels

Identify Any Skill Gaps or Redundancies

Compare your skills inventory against current and future business needs:

- Are there any critical skills missing?
- Are there areas where skills are duplicated unnecessarily?

Evaluate Employee Performance and Productivity

Review:

- Performance appraisal results
- Key performance indicators (KPIs)
- Productivity metrics specific to each role

Review Compensation and Benefits Structures

Analyze:

- Salary ranges for each position
- Bonus and incentive structures

- Benefits packages
- Comparison with industry standards

Assess Employee Satisfaction and Turnover Rates

Examine:

- Results from employee satisfaction surveys
- Exit interview feedback
- Turnover rates by department and position
- Length of tenure for employees

HR management software or even a well-organized spreadsheet can be useful for this process.

Technological Audit

Today, understanding your technological resources is crucial:

Inventory All Hardware

Create a comprehensive list of:

- Computers (desktops and laptops)
- Servers
- Mobile devices
- Networking equipment

- Printers and other peripherals

For each item, note:

- Make and model
- Age
- Specifications
- Current user or location

List All Software and Applications Used in the Business

Document:

- Operating systems
- Productivity suites
- Specialized software (e.g., design tools, CRM systems)
- Custom applications
- Cloud services

For each, include:

- Version number
- Number of licenses
- Renewal dates
- Integration with other systems

Assess the Age and Effectiveness of Your Technology

Evaluate:

- Performance of hardware against current needs
- Software version currency
- User satisfaction with current technology
- Compatibility issues

Identify Any Technology Gaps or Inefficiencies

Consider:

- Areas where manual processes could be automated
- Systems that don't integrate well
- Technology that's falling behind industry standards

Review Your Data Management and Security Practices

Assess:

- Data storage solutions
- Backup and recovery procedures
- Cybersecurity measures

- Compliance with relevant regulations (e.g., GDPR, HIPAA)

IT asset management tools can be helpful for larger businesses, while smaller ones might manage with a detailed inventory list.

Physical Asset Audit

This involves taking stock of all tangible assets:

Inventory of All Equipment and Machinery

Create a detailed list including:

- Production equipment
- Vehicles
- Office furniture
- Tools and small equipment

For each item, note:

- Purchase date and cost
- Current condition
- Maintenance history
- Expected lifespan

Review of Office or Retail Space

Assess:

- Total square footage
- Layout efficiency
- Utilization of space
- Lease terms (if applicable)
- Maintenance and utility costs

Assessment of Current Inventory Levels

For businesses carrying inventory:

- Conduct a physical count
- Compare actual stock levels to records
- Identify slow-moving or obsolete items
- Assess storage conditions

Evaluation of the Condition and Efficiency of Physical Assets

Consider:

- Age and condition of assets
- Maintenance requirements
- Energy efficiency
- Alignment with current business needs

For retail businesses, inventory management software can be particularly useful here.

SWOT Analysis

Once you've gathered all this information, it's time to put it into perspective with a SWOT analysis. SWOT stands for Strengths, Weaknesses, Opportunities, and Threats. This analysis helps you understand your internal capabilities (strengths and weaknesses) and external factors (opportunities and threats) that could impact your resource allocation decisions.

How to Conduct a SWOT Analysis

Strengths

Identify internal factors that give your organization an advantage. Consider:

- What resources do you have in abundance?
- What do you do better than your competitors?
- What unique resources or capabilities do you have?

Examples might include:

- Strong cash reserves

- Proprietary technology
- Highly skilled workforce
- Strong brand recognition

Weaknesses

Identify internal factors that put your organization at a disadvantage. Ask:

- Where are you resource-constrained?
- What resources do your competitors have that you don't?
- Where do you need to improve?

Examples could include:

- Outdated technology
- High employee turnover
- Limited production capacity
- Weak online presence

Opportunities

Identify external factors that your organization could capitalize on. Consider:

- Are there external changes that could benefit your business?

- Are there underserved markets you could tap into?
- Are there new technologies you could leverage?

Examples might include:

- Emerging markets
- Changes in customer preferences
- New distribution channels
- Potential for strategic partnerships

Threats

Identify external factors that could negatively impact your business. Ask:

- What external factors could negatively impact your business?
- Are there regulatory changes on the horizon?
- Are your competitors making moves that could threaten your position?

Examples could include:

- Increasing competition
- Economic downturns
- Changing regulations
- Technological disruption

Using SWOT Analysis for Resource Allocation

Once you've completed your SWOT analysis, use it to inform your resource allocation strategy:

1. Leverage Strengths: Allocate resources to areas where you're already strong to maintain or increase your competitive advantage.
2. Address Weaknesses: Identify which weaknesses are most critical and allocate resources to improve in these areas.
3. Capitalize on Opportunities: Ensure you have the necessary resources to take advantage of identified opportunities.
4. Mitigate Threats: Allocate resources to protect against or prepare for potential threats.

Remember, the SWOT analysis should be a dynamic tool. Revisit and update it regularly as your business and the external environment change.

Setting Baselines

The final step in assessing your current resources is to establish baselines. These are the metrics against which you'll measure future performance. Baselines serve several important purposes:

1. They provide a starting point for measuring progress
2. They help identify areas that need immediate attention
3. They allow for more accurate goal setting
4. They enable more effective performance tracking over time

Let's explore key baselines to consider in each area:

Financial Baselines

Revenue

- Total revenue
- Revenue by product or service line
- Revenue growth rate

Profit Margins

- Gross profit margin
- Operating profit margin
- Net profit margin

Cash Flow

- Operating cash flow
- Free cash flow

- Cash conversion cycle

Return on Investment

- ROI for different projects or initiatives
- ROI for marketing campaigns
- ROI for capital expenditures

Human Resource Baselines

Employee Productivity Metrics

- Revenue per employee
- Profit per employee
- Output per hour worked

Turnover Rates

- Overall turnover rate
- Voluntary vs. involuntary turnover
- Turnover by department or role

Employee Satisfaction Scores

- Overall employee satisfaction
- Satisfaction with specific aspects (e.g., compensation, work-life balance)
- Employee Net Promoter Score (eNPS)

Operational Baselines

Production Efficiency

- Units produced per hour
- Defect rate
- Equipment utilization rate

Customer Satisfaction Rates

- Customer satisfaction scores
- Net Promoter Score (NPS)
- Customer retention rate

Time-to-Market for New Products or Services

- Average development time
- Time from concept to launch
- Percentage of on-time launches

Technological Baselines

System Uptime

- Server uptime percentage
- Network availability
- Application availability

Software Utilization Rates

- Percentage of licenses used
- Frequency of software use
- User adoption rates for new technologies

Data Security Incident Rates

- Number of security breaches
- Time to detect and respond to incidents
- Percentage of employees complying with security policies

Analyzing Your Findings

After conducting your resource audit, establishing baselines, and performing a SWOT analysis, it's crucial to analyze your findings holistically. This analysis will form the foundation for your resource allocation strategy.

Key Questions to Consider

As you review your data, ask yourself:

1. Are our resources aligned with our business goals?
   - Look for discrepancies between where your resources are currently allocated and

where they need to be to achieve your strategic objectives.

2. Are there areas where we're over-resourced or under-resourced?
   ○ Identify any departments or functions that have more resources than necessary, as well as those that are struggling due to lack of resources.

3. What opportunities do we have to reallocate resources more effectively?
   ○ Consider how you might shift resources from areas of overabundance to areas of need.

4. How do our resource levels compare to industry benchmarks?
   ○ Research industry standards to understand how your resource allocation compares to competitors or best practices.

5. What are our most critical resource constraints?
   ○ Identify the resources that are most limiting your ability to achieve your goals.

6. How efficiently are we using our current resources?

○ Look for opportunities to improve efficiency and productivity with existing resources.

7. What risks do our current resource allocation patterns pose?

   ○ Consider potential vulnerabilities created by your current resource distribution.

8. How well are our resources positioned to capitalize on future opportunities?

   ○ Assess whether your current resources will be sufficient to take advantage of upcoming market trends or business opportunities.

Synthesizing Your Analysis

After considering these questions, synthesize your findings into a comprehensive view of your current resource situation. This synthesis should include:

1. An overview of your current resource allocation across all categories (financial, human, technological, physical)
2. A summary of key strengths and weaknesses in your resource portfolio

3. Identification of the most significant opportunities and threats related to your resources
4. A list of critical resource gaps that need to be addressed
5. Potential areas for resource reallocation or optimization
6. Recommendations for immediate actions to improve resource allocation

This analysis will serve as the foundation for your resource allocation strategy, which we'll start developing in the next chapter on strategic planning and goal setting.

Chapter 2 summary

Assessing your current resources is a critical first step in optimizing your resource allocation. By conducting a thorough audit, performing a SWOT analysis, and establishing baselines, you gain a comprehensive understanding of your resource landscape. This understanding allows you to identify strengths to leverage, weaknesses to address, opportunities to seize, and threats to mitigate.

Remember, this assessment process is not a one-time event. As your business evolves and the external environment changes, you'll need to regularly reassess your resources to ensure they remain aligned with your goals and strategies.

In the next chapter, we'll build on this foundation of understanding to develop a strategic approach to resource allocation, aligning your resources with your long-term business objectives.

Chapter 3: Strategic Planning and Goal Setting

Now that you have a clear picture of your current resources, it's time to look forward. Strategic planning and goal setting are crucial steps in effective resource allocation. They provide direction and purpose, ensuring that your resources are aligned with your business objectives.

By the end of this chapter, you'll be equipped with the knowledge and tools to align your day-to-day operations with your long-term vision, make informed decisions about resource allocation, and navigate the challenges that lie ahead. Let's begin by understanding the vital role of strategic planning in the business ecosystem.

The Importance of Strategic Planning

Defining Strategic Planning

Strategic planning is a systematic process that organizations undertake to define their direction and make decisions on allocating their resources to pursue this direction. It's the roadmap that bridges the gap between where a business currently stands and where it aspires to be in the future.

At its core, strategic planning involves:

1. Analyzing the current business environment
2. Identifying the organization's strengths, weaknesses, opportunities, and threats
3. Defining the company's mission, vision, and values
4. Setting long-term goals and objectives
5. Developing strategies to achieve these goals
6. Creating action plans to implement the strategies
7. Allocating resources effectively to support the plan
8. Establishing mechanisms to monitor progress and make adjustments as needed

The Critical Role of Strategic Planning in Resource Allocation

Strategic planning plays a pivotal role in effective resource allocation. Here's a detailed look at why it's crucial:

1. Provides Direction

A well-crafted strategic plan serves as a compass for your business, guiding all decisions and actions. It helps you:

- Clarify your business's purpose and long-term vision
- Align all departments and team members towards common goals
- Focus resources on activities that contribute directly to your objectives
- Avoid distractions and resource drain on non-essential activities

By providing a clear direction, strategic planning ensures that your resources are channeled towards what truly matters for your business's success.

2. Improves Decision Making

With a strategic plan in place, decision-making becomes more informed and less reactive. It enables you to:

- Evaluate opportunities and challenges against your strategic objectives
- Make resource allocation decisions based on long-term impact rather than short-term gains
- Justify and explain decisions to stakeholders with reference to the overall strategy
- Maintain consistency in decision-making across different levels of the organization

This improved decision-making process leads to more efficient use of resources and better overall outcomes for the business.

3. Enhances Coordination

Strategic planning fosters better coordination across different parts of your business:

- It creates a shared understanding of the company's goals and priorities
- Encourages cross-functional collaboration towards common objectives
- Helps identify and resolve potential conflicts in resource allocation
- Ensures that all departments are working in harmony rather than at cross-purposes

This enhanced coordination minimizes resource wastage and maximizes the impact of your allocation decisions.

4. Increases Efficiency

By focusing on strategic priorities, strategic planning helps increase overall business efficiency:

- It helps identify and eliminate activities that don't contribute to your strategic goals
- Encourages the optimization of processes to better serve your strategic objectives
- Allows for better resource utilization by aligning tasks with organizational goals
- Promotes a culture of continuous improvement aligned with your strategy

This focus on efficiency ensures that your resources are used in the most productive manner possible.

5. Prepares for Challenges

A good strategic plan doesn't just focus on opportunities; it also helps you anticipate and prepare for potential challenges:

- It encourages scenario planning, helping you prepare for different possible futures
- Allows you to allocate resources to build resilience and flexibility
- Helps identify potential risks and develop mitigation strategies
- Enables proactive rather than reactive resource allocation in the face of challenges

By preparing for challenges, strategic planning helps ensure that your resources are not just allocated effectively in the present, but are also positioned to handle future uncertainties.

The Strategic Planning Process

To harness these benefits, it's important to understand the strategic planning process. While the exact steps may vary depending on the organization, a typical process includes:

1. **Environmental Scanning**: Analyze the internal and external environment of your business. This includes market trends, competitive landscape, technological advancements, regulatory environment, and internal capabilities.
2. **Mission and Vision Formulation**: Define or refine your organization's mission (why you exist) and vision (where you want to go).
3. **Goal Setting**: Based on your mission and vision, set long-term goals for your organization.
4. **Strategy Formulation**: Develop strategies to achieve these goals. This involves making

high-level decisions about how you'll compete in the market and allocate your resources.

5. **Strategy Implementation**: Create detailed action plans to implement your strategies. This is where you decide on specific resource allocation.

6. **Monitoring and Evaluation**: Establish key performance indicators (KPIs) and processes to monitor your progress and evaluate the effectiveness of your strategies.

7. **Review and Adaptation**: Regularly review your strategic plan and adapt it as necessary based on changes in your business environment or performance.

By following this process, you create a comprehensive framework for effective resource allocation that aligns with your long-term business objectives.

SMART Goals: The Foundation of Effective Planning

Once you have a strategic plan in place, the next crucial step is to break it down into specific, actionable goals. This is where the concept of SMART goals comes into play. SMART is an acronym that stands for Specific, Measurable, Achievable, Relevant, and Time-bound. Let's explore each of these elements in detail.

Specific

The 'S' in SMART stands for Specific. A specific goal is clear, unambiguous, and leaves no room for misinterpretation. It answers the five 'W' questions:

- What do I want to accomplish?
- Why is this goal important?
- Who is involved?
- Where is it located?
- Which resources or limits are involved?

For example, instead of a vague goal like "increase sales," a specific goal might be "increase online sales of our flagship product by 20% in the North American market by expanding our digital marketing efforts."

Benefits of Specific Goals:

- Provides clear direction
- Makes it easier to create action plans
- Reduces misunderstandings among team members

- Increases motivation by clearly defining what success looks like

Tips for Making Goals Specific:

- Use action verbs
- Provide enough detail to remove ambiguity
- Focus on one outcome at a time
- Avoid generalities and vague language

Measurable

The 'M' in SMART stands for Measurable. A measurable goal allows you to track progress and know when you've achieved success. It answers questions like:

- How much?
- How many?
- How will I know when it is accomplished?

For instance, in our example of increasing online sales by 20%, the 20% increase is the measurable element.

Benefits of Measurable Goals:

- Allows for objective assessment of progress
- Provides motivation as you see progress

- Helps in determining when a goal has been achieved
- Allows for course correction if progress is off track

Tips for Making Goals Measurable:

- Attach a number or percentage to your goal
- Define specific criteria for measuring progress
- Use tools or systems to track progress
- Set milestones along the way to your final goal

Achievable

The 'A' in SMART stands for Achievable. While goals should be challenging, they also need to be realistic given your resources and constraints. An achievable goal answers questions like:

- How can I accomplish this goal?
- Do I have the necessary resources and capabilities?
- Have others done it successfully before?

Benefits of Achievable Goals:

- Prevents setting yourself up for failure
- Maintains motivation and morale

- Ensures efficient use of resources
- Builds confidence as you achieve your goals

Tips for Making Goals Achievable:

- Consider your available resources (time, money, skills)
- Research similar goals others have achieved
- Break larger goals into smaller, more manageable steps
- Be honest about potential obstacles

Relevant

The 'R' in SMART stands for Relevant. Your goals should align with your broader business objectives and strategy. A relevant goal answers "yes" to these questions:

- Does this seem worthwhile?
- Is this the right time?
- Does this match our other efforts/needs?
- Is it applicable in the current socio-economic environment?

Benefits of Relevant Goals:

- Ensures alignment with your overall business strategy
- Prevents wasting resources on non-essential activities
- Increases buy-in from stakeholders
- Contributes directly to your long-term success

Tips for Making Goals Relevant:

- Align goals with your mission and vision
- Consider how the goal fits into your overall business plan
- Ensure the goal is within your control or influence
- Consider the current business climate and market trends

Time-bound

The 'T' in SMART stands for Time-bound. Every goal should have a deadline or timeframe. This creates urgency and helps you prioritize. A time-bound goal answers questions like:

- When?
- What can I do six months from now?
- What can I do six weeks from now?

- What can I do today?

In our example, the goal might become "increase online sales of our flagship product by 20% by the end of Q3."

Benefits of Time-bound Goals:

- Creates a sense of urgency
- Helps in prioritizing tasks
- Prevents goals from being overtaken by daily tasks
- Allows for better planning and resource allocation

Tips for Making Goals Time-bound:

- Set a specific deadline
- Break long-term goals into shorter-term milestones
- Be realistic about the time needed to achieve the goal
- Consider factors that might affect your timeline

Examples of SMART Goals for Different Business Areas

Let's explore some examples of SMART goals for various areas of a small business:

Financial

- "Reduce operating costs by 10% within the next 6 months without compromising product quality or customer service."
- "Increase profit margins by 5% over the next fiscal year by optimizing our pricing strategy and reducing production costs."

Human Resources

- "Implement a new employee training program that increases productivity by 15% within 1 year."
- "Reduce employee turnover rate from 20% to 15% by the end of the next fiscal year through improved onboarding and employee engagement initiatives."

Marketing

- "Launch a social media campaign that increases website traffic by 30% over the next quarter."

- "Improve customer retention rate from 70% to 80% within the next 12 months by implementing a customer loyalty program."

Product Development

- "Develop and launch two new products that each generate $100,000 in revenue within their first year on the market."
- "Reduce product development cycle time by 20% over the next 18 months by streamlining our design and testing processes."

Operations

- "Improve on-time delivery rate from 85% to 95% within the next 6 months by optimizing our supply chain and logistics processes."
- "Reduce waste in the production process by 25% over the next year through the implementation of lean manufacturing principles."

Customer Service

- "Increase customer satisfaction scores from 7.5 to 8.5 out of 10 within the next 12 months by providing additional training to our customer service team."

- "Reduce average customer response time from 24 hours to 12 hours by the end of Q2 through the implementation of a new customer service software."

Sales

- "Increase the average deal size by 15% over the next 6 months by focusing on upselling and cross-selling strategies."
- "Expand into two new geographical markets by the end of the year, generating at least $500,000 in new revenue."

Each of these goals follows the SMART criteria, providing a clear target for the business to work towards. They specify what needs to be achieved, how it will be measured, ensure it's achievable, align with broader business objectives, and set a clear timeframe.

Prioritizing Objectives

After setting your SMART goals, you're likely to find yourself with more objectives than you can realistically pursue at once. This is where the crucial skill of prioritization comes into play. Prioritizing your objectives ensures that you're focusing your limited resources on the goals that will have the most significant impact on your business.

Strategies for Prioritizing Objectives

Let's explore some effective strategies for prioritizing your business objectives:

1. Short-term vs. Long-term Goals

One of the first considerations in prioritizing objectives is the timeframe. Both short-term and long-term goals have their place in a balanced business strategy.

Short-term Goals:

- Address immediate needs or quick wins
- Provide momentum and immediate results
- Help maintain cash flow and operational stability
- Can boost team morale by showing progress

Long-term Goals:

- Focus on sustained success and growth

- Often require more significant resource investment
- Shape the future direction of the business
- Build long-term competitive advantages

Balancing Short-term and Long-term Goals:

- Aim for a mix of both to ensure current operations and future growth
- Use short-term goals to build towards long-term objectives
- Ensure long-term goals don't compromise short-term stability
- Regularly reassess the balance based on business performance and market conditions

2. High-impact vs. Low-impact Activities

Not all activities are created equal when it comes to their impact on your business. The Pareto Principle, also known as the 80/20 rule, suggests that 80% of your results come from 20% of your efforts.

Identifying High-impact Activities:

- Analyze past performance data to identify activities that drove significant results

- Consider activities that directly contribute to your key performance indicators (KPIs)
- Look for activities that address critical business needs or market demands
- Identify tasks that have a multiplier effect, positively impacting multiple areas of the business

Dealing with Low-impact Activities:

- Evaluate if low-impact activities can be eliminated without negative consequences
- Consider outsourcing or automating low-impact but necessary tasks
- Look for ways to streamline or combine low-impact activities to increase efficiency

Applying the Pareto Principle:

- Focus the majority of your resources on the high-impact 20% of activities
- Regularly review and adjust your assessment of high-impact activities as business conditions change
- Train your team to identify and prioritize high-impact tasks in their daily work

3. Urgency vs. Importance: The Eisenhower Matrix

The Eisenhower Matrix, named after President Dwight D. Eisenhower, is a powerful tool for prioritizing tasks based on their urgency and importance. It divides tasks into four quadrants:

1. Urgent and Important:

- These tasks require immediate attention and have significant consequences
- Examples: Crises, pressing problems, deadline-driven projects
- Action: Do these tasks immediately

2. Important but Not Urgent:

- These tasks contribute to long-term goals and values but don't require immediate action
- Examples: Strategic planning, relationship building, personal development
- Action: Schedule these tasks and allocate dedicated time for them

3. Urgent but Not Important:

- These tasks demand attention but don't contribute significantly to your goals
- Examples: Some meetings, some phone calls, some emails
- Action: Delegate these tasks if possible, or handle them quickly

4. Neither Urgent nor Important:

- These tasks don't contribute to your goals and aren't time-sensitive
- Examples: Time wasters, trivial tasks, some forms of entertainment
- Action: Eliminate these tasks whenever possible

Implementing the Eisenhower Matrix:

- Regularly categorize your tasks and goals into these four quadrants
- Focus most of your energy on Quadrant 2 (Important but Not Urgent) for long-term success
- Develop systems to handle Quadrant 1 (Urgent and Important) tasks efficiently
- Minimize time spent on Quadrant 3 and 4 tasks

4. Resource Availability

When prioritizing objectives, it's crucial to consider the resources you have available. This includes financial resources, human capital, time, and technological capabilities.

Assessing Resource Availability:

- Conduct a thorough inventory of your current resources
- Consider potential resource constraints or limitations
- Identify any underutilized resources that could be redirected

Matching Goals to Resources:

- Prioritize goals that align well with your current resource strengths
- Consider deferring resource-intensive goals until you've built up necessary capabilities
- Look for goals that can leverage existing resources in new ways

Resource Allocation Strategies:

- Consider the concept of opportunity cost when allocating resources

- Use techniques like zero-based budgeting to ensure resources are allocated based on current priorities, not historical patterns
- Implement a resource management system to track and optimize resource utilization

5. Dependencies

Some goals may be dependent on the completion of others. Understanding these dependencies is crucial for effective prioritization.

Identifying Dependencies:

- Map out the relationships between different goals and projects
- Identify any goals that serve as foundations or enablers for others
- Consider both direct and indirect dependencies

Managing Dependencies:

- Prioritize foundational goals that will enable future success
- Use project management tools to visualize and manage complex dependencies
- Build flexibility into your plans to account for potential delays in dependent tasks

**

6. Risk vs. Reward:

- Consider the potential upside of each goal against the resources required and the risk involved.
- High-risk, high-reward goals might be worth pursuing, but balance them with more certain objectives.

7. Alignment with Core Strategy:

- Prioritize goals that align most closely with your overall business strategy and vision.

Remember, prioritization isn't a one-time activity. As your business environment changes and you make progress on your goals, you'll need to regularly reassess and reprioritize.

By the end of this process, you should have a clear set of prioritized, SMART goals that align with your overall business strategy. These goals will guide your resource allocation decisions, ensuring that you're investing your limited resources where they can have the biggest impact.

In the next chapter, we'll dive into one of the most critical areas of resource allocation for small businesses: financial resource allocation. We'll explore budgeting, cash flow management, and investment analysis to help you make the most of your financial resources.

Chapter 4: Financial Resource Allocation for Small Businesses

Financial resources are often the most constrained and most critical for small businesses. How you allocate your financial resources can make the difference between thriving and merely surviving. In this chapter, we'll explore key aspects of financial resource allocation: budgeting, cash flow management, and investment analysis. These elements form the cornerstone of effective financial management for small businesses, enabling them to navigate economic challenges, seize growth opportunities, and build a sustainable future.

The Importance of Financial Resource Allocation

Before delving into the specifics of budgeting, cash flow management, and investment analysis, it's crucial to understand why financial resource allocation is so vital for small businesses:

1. **Limited Resources**: Small businesses typically have fewer financial resources than larger

corporations. This scarcity makes it imperative to allocate every dollar wisely.

2. **Competitive Advantage**: Efficient allocation of financial resources can give small businesses a competitive edge, allowing them to respond quickly to market changes and customer needs.

3. **Risk Management**: Proper financial resource allocation helps mitigate risks by ensuring the business has adequate reserves and is not overly exposed in any one area.

4. **Growth and Expansion**: Strategic allocation of finances enables small businesses to invest in growth opportunities, whether it's expanding product lines, entering new markets, or improving infrastructure.

5. **Sustainability**: Effective financial management ensures the long-term viability of the business, helping it weather economic downturns and capitalize on upswings.

Creating a Budget

A budget is a financial plan for a defined period, usually a year. It's an estimate of revenue and expenses over this period. Budgeting is crucial for several reasons:

- It provides a roadmap for your financial decisions.
- It helps you prepare for lean periods.
- It allows you to plan for growth and expansion.
- It helps you identify potential financial problems before they occur.

Steps to Create an Effective Budget

1. Review Your Revenue Sources

- List all your income streams
- Analyze past performance and trends
- Consider factors that might impact future revenue (market conditions, new products, etc.)

When reviewing your revenue sources, it's important to be both realistic and comprehensive. Start by listing all current income streams, including sales of products or services, investment income, and any other sources of revenue. Then, analyze the performance of each stream over the past few years. Look for trends: Are certain products or services growing in popularity? Are others declining?

Next, consider external factors that might impact your future revenue. This could include:

- Changes in the overall economy
- Shifts in your industry or market
- New competitors entering the market
- Technological advancements that could disrupt your business model
- Changes in consumer behavior or preferences

By thoroughly understanding your revenue sources and the factors that influence them, you can make more accurate projections for your budget.

2. Estimate Your Expenses

- Fixed costs (rent, salaries, insurance, etc.)
- Variable costs (materials, utilities, commissions, etc.)
- One-time expenses (equipment purchases, renovations, etc.)

Estimating expenses accurately is crucial for creating a realistic budget. Start by categorizing your expenses:

Fixed Costs: These are expenses that remain relatively constant regardless of your business's performance. Examples include:

- Rent or mortgage payments
- Salaries for full-time employees

- Insurance premiums
- Loan repayments

Variable Costs: These expenses fluctuate based on your business activity. They might include:

- Raw materials or inventory
- Utilities
- Shipping costs
- Sales commissions

One-time Expenses: These are non-recurring costs that you anticipate in the coming year, such as:

- Major equipment purchases
- Office renovations
- Software upgrades
- Legal or consulting fees for special projects

When estimating expenses, review your past financial records and consider any anticipated changes. For example, are you planning to hire new employees? Will your rent increase when your lease renews? Are raw material costs expected to rise?

3. Set Financial Goals

- Align with your SMART goals from the previous chapter
- Include targets for revenue, profit margins, and growth

Your budget should reflect your business's overall strategic goals. Refer back to the SMART goals you set in the previous chapter and ensure your budget aligns with these objectives. Some financial goals you might include are:

- Increase revenue by X% compared to the previous year
- Improve profit margins by Y percentage points
- Reduce overhead costs by Z%
- Achieve a specific return on investment for new projects
- Build up cash reserves to cover X months of operating expenses

Make sure your goals are specific, measurable, achievable, relevant, and time-bound (SMART). This will make it easier to track your progress and make adjustments as needed.

4. Create Your Budget

- Use a spreadsheet or budgeting software
- Break down revenue and expenses by month
- Include a contingency fund for unexpected expenses

With your revenue projections, expense estimates, and financial goals in hand, you're ready to create your budget. Here's how to proceed:

1. Choose your tool: A spreadsheet program like Microsoft Excel or Google Sheets can work well for many small businesses. There are also specialized budgeting software options available that can offer more features and automation.
2. Set up your spreadsheet: Create columns for each month of the year, plus a total column. Create rows for each revenue stream and expense category.
3. Enter your projections: Based on your analysis, enter your projected revenue and expenses for each month. Be as detailed as possible.
4. Calculate totals: Use formulas to calculate monthly and annual totals for revenue, expenses, and profit (revenue minus expenses).
5. Create a contingency fund: Set aside a portion of your projected revenue (typically 5-10%) as a

contingency fund for unexpected expenses or revenue shortfalls.

6. Compare to goals: Check if your budget aligns with the financial goals you set. If not, you may need to adjust your projections or reconsider your goals.

5. Review and Adjust

- Compare actual results to your budget regularly
- Adjust your budget as needed based on performance and changing conditions

Remember, a budget is a living document. It should be flexible enough to adapt to changing circumstances while still providing a clear financial roadmap. Here's how to keep your budget relevant and useful:

1. Regular reviews: Set aside time each month to compare your actual financial performance to your budget projections.
2. Analyze variances: For any significant differences between actual and budgeted amounts, try to understand why. Was it a one-time event, or does it indicate a trend?

3. Make adjustments: Based on your analysis, update your budget projections for the remaining months of the year. This might involve adjusting revenue projections, cutting costs, or reallocating resources.
4. Learn and improve: Use the insights gained from your budget reviews to improve your budgeting process for the next year.

Cash Flow Management

Cash flow - the movement of money in and out of your business - is critical for small businesses. Even profitable companies can fail due to poor cash flow management. Here are some techniques for effective cash flow management:

Create a Cash Flow Forecast

- Project your cash inflows and outflows for the coming months
- Identify potential cash shortfalls in advance

A cash flow forecast is similar to a budget, but it focuses specifically on the timing of cash movements. Here's how to create one:

1. Start with your current cash balance.

2. List expected cash inflows (customer payments, loans, etc.) for each week or month.
3. List expected cash outflows (bill payments, payroll, loan repayments, etc.) for each period.
4. Calculate your net cash flow (inflows minus outflows) for each period.
5. Update your cash balance at the end of each period.

This forecast will help you identify periods where you might face cash shortages, allowing you to take preventive action.

Manage Receivables

- Invoice promptly and accurately
- Offer incentives for early payment
- Follow up on overdue payments quickly

Effective management of accounts receivable is crucial for maintaining healthy cash flow. Here are some strategies:

1. **Prompt invoicing**: Send invoices as soon as goods or services are delivered. Consider using electronic invoicing to speed up the process.

2. **Clear payment terms**: Ensure your invoices clearly state payment due dates and accepted payment methods.
3. **Early payment incentives**: Offer a small discount (e.g., 2%) for payments made within a short period (e.g., 10 days).
4. **Late payment penalties**: Consider charging interest on overdue payments to encourage timely payment.
5. **Regular follow-ups**: Implement a system for following up on overdue payments. This could involve automated reminders followed by personal phone calls for seriously overdue accounts.
6. **Credit checks**: For new customers or large orders, consider running credit checks to assess the risk of non-payment.

Negotiate with Suppliers

- Try to extend payment terms where possible
- Look for early payment discounts

Your relationships with suppliers can significantly impact your cash flow. Consider these strategies:

1. **Extended payment terms**: Negotiate longer payment terms with your suppliers. This allows you to hold onto your cash longer.
2. **Early payment discounts**: Some suppliers offer discounts for early payment. Calculate whether these discounts provide a better return than holding onto your cash.
3. **Volume discounts**: If you can accurately forecast your needs, consider buying in bulk to secure discounts.
4. **Consignment arrangements**: For certain types of inventory, suppliers might agree to consignment arrangements where you only pay for items after you've sold them.
5. **Open communication**: Keep your suppliers informed about your business's situation. If you anticipate difficulty making a payment, it's better to communicate this in advance and potentially negotiate a solution.

Manage Inventory

- Don't tie up too much cash in inventory
- Use just-in-time inventory methods where appropriate

Inventory represents cash that's tied up and unavailable for other uses. Efficient inventory management can significantly improve your cash flow:

1. **Just-in-time (JIT) inventory**: This approach involves ordering inventory only as it's needed, reducing the amount of cash tied up in stock.
2. **ABC analysis**: Categorize your inventory into A (high value, low quantity), B (moderate value and quantity), and C (low value, high quantity) items. Focus your management efforts on A items.
3. **Economic Order Quantity (EOQ)**: Use this formula to determine the optimal order quantity that minimizes total inventory costs.
4. **Regular stock takes**: Conduct regular inventory counts to ensure your records are accurate and to identify slow-moving or obsolete stock.
5. **Dropshipping**: For some products, consider dropshipping arrangements where the supplier ships directly to your customer, eliminating the need for you to hold inventory.

Consider a Line of Credit

- This can help smooth out cash flow fluctuations
- Use it strategically, not as a long-term solution

A line of credit can be a valuable tool for managing cash flow, but it should be used judiciously:

1. **Understand the terms**: Make sure you're clear on the interest rate, repayment terms, and any fees associated with the line of credit.
2. **Use for short-term needs**: A line of credit is best used to cover short-term cash flow gaps, not for long-term financing needs.
3. **Have a repayment plan**: Whenever you draw on your line of credit, have a clear plan for when and how you'll repay it.
4. **Monitor your usage**: Regularly review your use of the line of credit. If you find you're consistently maxing it out, this could indicate deeper financial issues that need addressing.
5. **Shop around**: Don't automatically accept the first offer from your bank. Shop around for the best terms and rates.

Time Major Purchases Carefully

- Align large expenditures with periods of strong cash flow

When planning major purchases or investments:

1. Use your cash flow forecast to identify periods of strong positive cash flow.
2. Try to time large expenditures to coincide with these periods.
3. If a purchase can't wait, consider financing options that align repayments with your cash flow patterns.
4. For very large purchases, consider breaking them into smaller phases if possible.

Monitor Cash Flow Regularly

- Review your cash position at least weekly
- Use cash flow management tools or software

Regular monitoring is key to effective cash flow management:

1. **Weekly reviews**: At a minimum, review your cash position weekly. This includes checking bank balances, upcoming payables and receivables, and any unusual transactions.

2. **Use technology**: Consider using cash flow management software that can automate much of the tracking and provide visual representations of your cash flow.
3. **Key Performance Indicators (KPIs)**: Monitor cash flow-related KPIs such as Days Sales Outstanding (DSO), Days Payables Outstanding (DPO), and cash conversion cycle.
4. **Bank reconciliations**: Regularly reconcile your bank statements with your accounting records to ensure accuracy.
5. **Cash flow statements**: Generate and review cash flow statements monthly to understand the sources and uses of your cash.

Investment and Cost-Benefit Analysis

When it comes to allocating financial resources to new projects or investments, it's crucial to conduct thorough analysis to ensure you're making the best use of your limited funds.

Evaluating Investment Opportunities

a) Return on Investment (ROI)

- Calculate the expected return for each dollar invested
- ROI = (Net Profit / Cost of Investment) x 100

Return on Investment is a fundamental metric for evaluating the profitability of an investment:

1. **Calculate net profit**: This is the total revenue generated by the investment minus all associated costs.
2. **Determine investment cost**: Include all costs related to the investment, including initial purchase, implementation costs, and ongoing expenses.
3. **Calculate ROI**: Divide net profit by investment cost and multiply by 100 to get a percentage.
4. **Interpret the result**: A higher ROI indicates a more profitable investment. However, ROI should be considered alongside other factors like risk and alignment with business strategy.
5. **Consider time frame**: ROI can vary significantly depending on the time frame considered. Be sure to calculate and compare ROI over consistent time periods.

b) Payback Period

- How long will it take to recoup the initial investment?
- Shorter payback periods are generally preferable

The payback period is the time it takes for an investment to generate enough cash flow to recover its initial cost:

1. **Calculate annual cash inflows**: Determine how much additional cash the investment will generate each year.
2. **Divide initial investment by annual cash inflow**: This gives you the payback period in years.
3. **Consider the time value of money**: For more accuracy, you can use discounted cash flows to calculate the discounted payback period.
4. **Compare to your threshold**: Determine what payback period is acceptable for your business. Investments with shorter payback periods are generally considered less risky.
5. **Limitations**: Remember that payback period doesn't account for cash flows beyond the

payback period or the time value of money (unless you use the discounted method).

c) Net Present Value (NPV)

- Accounts for the time value of money
- Positive NPV indicates a potentially good investment

Net Present Value is a more sophisticated method that takes into account the time value of money:

1. **Project future cash flows**: Estimate the cash inflows and outflows for each period of the investment's life.
2. **Determine discount rate**: This is the rate used to discount future cash flows to their present value. It often represents the company's cost of capital.
3. **Calculate present value of cash flows**: Use the discount rate to calculate the present value of each future cash flow.
4. **Sum present values**: Add up all the discounted cash flows.
5. **Subtract initial investment**: The result is the NPV.

6. **Interpret the result**: A positive NPV indicates that the investment is expected to add value to the company. A negative NPV suggests the investment may destroy value.

d) Internal Rate of Return (IRR)

- The discount rate that makes the NPV of all cash flows equal to zero
- Higher IRR generally indicates a more desirable investment

IRR is closely related to NPV:

1. **Calculate IRR**: This is typically done using financial software or spreadsheet functions, as it involves complex iterations.
2. **Compare to hurdle rate**: The hurdle rate is the minimum acceptable rate of return for investments. If the IRR exceeds the hurdle rate, the investment may be worthwhile.
3. **Consider alongside NPV**: IRR can be a useful complement to NPV, but it has limitations, particularly when comparing mutually exclusive projects.
4. **Be aware of multiple IRRs**: In some cases, particularly with non-conventional cash flows,

there may be multiple IRRs, which can complicate interpretation.

Performing Cost-Benefit Analysis

a) Identify All Costs

- Direct costs (materials, labor, etc.)
- Indirect costs (overhead, opportunity costs, etc.)

A thorough cost-benefit analysis starts with identifying all relevant costs:

1. **Direct costs**: These are costs directly attributable to the project or investment. Examples include:
   - Materials and supplies
   - Labor costs for employees working directly on the project
   - Equipment or technology purchases
   - Training costs
   - Marketing expenses specific to the project
2. **Indirect costs**: These are costs that are not directly tied to the project but are necessary for its completion. They might include:
   - Overhead costs (rent, utilities, insurance)

- Administrative support
- Maintenance and repairs
- Compliance costs

3. **Opportunity costs**: Consider what you're giving up by pursuing this investment. For example, if you're allocating resources to this project, what other opportunities are you missing?

4. **Future costs**: Don't forget to consider ongoing costs that may arise after the initial implementation. These could include:
   - Maintenance and upgrades
   - Additional staffing needs
   - Increased insurance premiums
   - Regulatory compliance costs

5. **Hidden costs**: Be thorough in identifying less obvious costs such as:
   - Potential disruptions to existing operations
   - Employee resistance or reduced productivity during transition periods
   - Potential environmental impact costs
   - Costs associated with risk mitigation

b) Identify All Benefits

- Tangible benefits (increased revenue, cost savings)
- Intangible benefits (improved brand image, employee satisfaction)

Just as important as identifying costs is recognizing all potential benefits:

1. **Tangible benefits**: These are benefits that can be easily quantified in monetary terms. Examples include:
   - Increased revenue from new products or markets
   - Cost savings from improved efficiency
   - Reduced waste or improved resource utilization
   - Lower maintenance costs
   - Improved cash flow
2. **Intangible benefits**: While harder to quantify, these benefits can be crucial to long-term success. They might include:
   - Enhanced brand reputation or market position
   - Improved customer satisfaction and loyalty
   - Better employee morale and retention

- Increased flexibility or scalability of operations
- Improved compliance or risk management
- Knowledge acquisition or improved organizational capabilities

3. **Competitive advantages**: Consider how the investment might strengthen your position relative to competitors:
   - First-mover advantages in new markets
   - Proprietary technology or processes
   - Improved ability to attract top talent

4. **Long-term strategic benefits**: Some benefits may not be immediate but could be crucial for long-term success:
   - Positioning for future growth opportunities
   - Building relationships with key partners or customers
   - Developing capabilities that may be critical in the future

c) Assign Monetary Values

- Quantify benefits and costs in financial terms where possible

This step involves converting both costs and benefits into monetary terms to allow for direct comparison:

1. **Direct conversion**: For many tangible costs and benefits, this is straightforward. Use market prices, salary data, or other readily available financial information.
2. **Estimating intangibles**: For less tangible items, you may need to use estimation techniques:
   - Market research to estimate the value of improved brand image
   - HR data to estimate the cost savings from improved employee retention
   - Industry benchmarks to estimate efficiency improvements
3. **Scenario analysis**: When exact values are hard to determine, consider creating multiple scenarios (best case, worst case, most likely) to get a range of potential values.
4. **Time value of money**: Remember to account for the timing of costs and benefits. A dollar today is worth more than a dollar in the future, so use discounting techniques for future cash flows.

5. **Sensitivity analysis**: Test how your results change when you adjust key assumptions. This can help you understand which factors have the biggest impact on the overall analysis.

d) Compare Costs and Benefits

- Calculate the benefit-cost ratio
- Consider both short-term and long-term impacts

Now that you've quantified costs and benefits, it's time to compare them:

1. **Net benefit calculation**: Subtract total costs from total benefits to get the net benefit.
2. **Benefit-cost ratio**: Divide total benefits by total costs. A ratio greater than 1 indicates that benefits outweigh costs.
3. **Payback period**: Calculate how long it will take for the cumulative benefits to exceed the costs.
4. **NPV and IRR**: If you're considering a long-term project, calculate the Net Present Value and Internal Rate of Return as discussed earlier.
5. **Short-term vs. long-term**: Consider both immediate impacts and long-term effects. Some

investments might have negative short-term returns but significant long-term benefits.

6. **Risk-adjusted return**: Consider adjusting your calculations based on the level of risk associated with achieving the benefits.

e) Consider Non-Financial Factors

- Strategic fit
- Risk factors
- Regulatory compliance

While financial analysis is crucial, it shouldn't be the only factor in your decision-making:

1. **Strategic alignment**: How well does the investment align with your overall business strategy and goals? Even a profitable project might not be worth pursuing if it doesn't fit with your long-term vision.
2. **Risk assessment**: Consider the potential downsides and their likelihood:
   - Market risks (changes in customer preferences, competitive actions)
   - Operational risks (implementation challenges, dependencies on key personnel)

- Financial risks (cost overruns, currency fluctuations)
- Regulatory risks (changes in laws or regulations)

3. **Regulatory compliance**: Ensure that the investment doesn't create compliance issues. In some cases, investments might be necessary to meet regulatory requirements.

4. **Ethical considerations**: Consider the ethical implications of the investment. How might it impact your stakeholders, the environment, or the broader community?

5. **Organizational impact**: How will the investment affect your company culture, employee morale, or operational processes?

6. **Opportunity cost**: Consider what other opportunities you might be foregoing by pursuing this investment.

7. **Timing and market conditions**: Is this the right time for this investment given current market conditions and your company's situation?

Chapter 4 summary

Effective financial resource allocation is a critical skill for small business success. By implementing robust budgeting practices, managing cash flow diligently, and carefully analyzing potential investments, you can make the most of your limited financial resources.

Remember that budgeting and financial planning are ongoing processes. Regular review and adjustment are necessary to keep your financial strategy aligned with your business goals and market realities. Be prepared to make tough decisions, whether it's cutting costs in certain areas or making strategic investments for future growth.

While financial considerations are crucial, they should always be balanced with other strategic factors. The most successful small businesses are those that can align their financial decisions with their overall business strategy, market positioning, and long-term vision.

In the next chapter, we'll explore another critical area of resource allocation: human resources. We'll discuss strategies for hiring, developing, and retaining the right people to drive your business forward. Remember, while financial resources are vital, it's often the human resources that truly differentiate successful small businesses from their competitors.

Chapter 5: Human Resource Allocation

Human Resource Allocation resources are often described as a company's most valuable asset, and for good reason. The skills, knowledge, and efforts of your team can make or break your business. Effective allocation of human resources is crucial for maximizing productivity, fostering innovation, and achieving your business goals. Let's explore key aspects of human resource allocation in depth.

Hiring the Right People

The first step in human resource allocation is ensuring you have the right people on your team. This involves developing effective recruitment strategies, balancing skill requirements with cultural fit, and implementing a robust hiring process.

Recruitment Strategies

a) Define the Role Clearly

Before beginning the recruitment process, it's crucial to have a clear understanding of the role you're trying to fill. This involves:

- Creating detailed job descriptions that outline responsibilities, required qualifications, and expected outcomes
- Identifying must-have skills versus nice-to-have skills
- Considering how the role fits into your overall organizational structure and contributes to business goals

A well-defined role helps attract suitable candidates and sets clear expectations from the start.

b) Source Candidates Creatively

While traditional job boards are still useful, consider diversifying your candidate sourcing methods:

- Employee referrals: Encourage your current employees to refer qualified candidates. This can lead to better cultural fits and reduced hiring costs.
- Professional networks: Leverage platforms like LinkedIn to connect with potential candidates directly.
- Social media platforms: Use social media to showcase your company culture and attract passive candidates.

- Industry events: Attend or host industry events to meet potential candidates in person.
- Partnerships with educational institutions: Build relationships with universities or trade schools to access fresh talent.

c) Streamline the Application Process

A cumbersome application process can deter qualified candidates. Consider the following:

- Make it easy for candidates to apply through your website or mobile devices
- Use applicant tracking systems (ATS) for larger hiring efforts to manage applications efficiently
- Provide clear instructions and set expectations about the hiring timeline

d) Conduct Thorough Interviews

The interview process is crucial for assessing candidates' suitability. Consider implementing:

- Structured interviews: Use a consistent set of questions for all candidates to ensure fair comparisons

- Practical tests or work samples: Where appropriate, include job-related tasks or simulations to assess skills
- Multiple interviewers: Involve team members and potential colleagues to get diverse perspectives
- Behavioral interviewing techniques: Ask candidates to provide specific examples of past behavior to predict future performance

Hiring for Skill vs. Cultural Fit

Both skills and cultural fit are important, but their relative importance may vary depending on the role and your business needs.

a) Skills Assessment

When evaluating skills, consider:

- Technical skills required for the job: These are often non-negotiable requirements
- Soft skills like communication, problem-solving, and adaptability: These are increasingly important in most roles
- Current skills vs. potential for growth: Sometimes, a candidate's potential and learning

ability can be more valuable than their current skill set

Implement skill assessment methods such as:

- Technical interviews or coding challenges for technical roles
- Writing samples or presentations for communication-heavy positions
- Situational judgment tests to assess problem-solving and decision-making skills

b) Cultural Fit Evaluation

Assessing cultural fit involves considering:

- Alignment with company values and work style: Does the candidate's work ethic and approach align with your company's culture?
- Ability to work well with the existing team: Will they complement or clash with current team dynamics?
- Long-term potential within the organization: Could you see this person growing with your company?

Methods to assess cultural fit include:

- Behavioral interview questions focused on past experiences and how they align with your company values
- Team interviews to see how the candidate interacts with potential colleagues
- Trial periods or project-based hiring to observe the candidate in action

Strive for a balance between skills and cultural fit. A candidate with a perfect skill set but poor cultural fit may struggle to integrate and be productive. Conversely, someone who fits in well but lacks essential skills may not be able to perform the job effectively.

Employee Development

Once you have the right people on board, it's crucial to invest in their development. This not only improves their performance but also increases retention and job satisfaction.

Training and Development Programs

a) Onboarding

A comprehensive onboarding process sets new hires up for success:

- Provide a thorough introduction to the company, its culture, and values
- Clearly communicate job expectations, goals, and performance metrics
- Introduce new hires to key team members and stakeholders
- Provide necessary tools, resources, and access to systems
- Assign a mentor or buddy to help with integration

b) Ongoing Training

Continuous learning is essential in today's rapidly changing business environment:

- Offer regular skills updates and opportunities for new skill acquisition
- Provide both technical and soft skills training
- Use a mix of learning methods: in-person workshops, online courses, mentoring, job rotation
- Encourage employees to attend industry conferences or seminars
- Implement a learning management system (LMS) to track and manage training

c) Leadership Development

Identifying and nurturing future leaders is crucial for long-term success:

- Create a leadership pipeline by identifying high-potential employees
- Offer leadership training programs focusing on skills like strategic thinking, decision-making, and people management
- Provide mentoring and coaching opportunities with senior leaders
- Offer stretch assignments to challenge and develop leadership skills
- Consider implementing a formal succession planning process

Retention Strategies

Retaining top talent is often more cost-effective than constant recruitment. Consider the following strategies:

a) Competitive Compensation

Ensure your compensation packages remain competitive:

- Conduct regular market rate reviews for all positions
- Implement performance-based bonuses or raises
- Consider equity or profit-sharing programs for key employees

b) Benefits Package

Offer a comprehensive benefits package that addresses diverse employee needs:

- Health insurance, including mental health coverage
- Retirement plans with company matching
- Paid time off, including vacation, sick leave, and personal days
- Consider flexible benefits that employees can choose from based on their needs

c) Work-Life Balance

Promoting work-life balance can significantly improve employee satisfaction and retention:

- Offer flexible working hours or remote work options where possible

- Ensure adequate vacation time and encourage employees to use it
- Implement policies to prevent burnout, such as no-email hours or meeting-free days
- Offer wellness programs or gym memberships

d) Career Growth Opportunities

Employees often leave when they can't see a future with the company:

- Provide clear career progression paths for all roles
- Offer internal promotion opportunities before external hiring
- Support lateral moves for employees wanting to explore different areas of the business
- Provide education assistance for relevant degrees or certifications

e) Recognition and Appreciation

Regular recognition can significantly boost morale and retention:

- Implement a formal employee recognition program

- Provide regular feedback through performance reviews and informal check-ins
- Celebrate both individual and team achievements
- Consider non-monetary rewards like extra time off or choice of projects

Delegation and Task Management

Effective delegation and task management are crucial for making the most of your human resources.

Effective Delegation Techniques

a) Choose the Right Person

Match tasks to skills and development needs:

- Consider both current capabilities and growth potential
- Use delegation as a development tool for high-potential employees
- Ensure the delegated task aligns with the employee's career goals where possible

b) Provide Clear Instructions

Clear communication is key to successful delegation:

- Clearly articulate expectations, deadlines, and desired outcomes
- Provide context for why the task is important and how it fits into larger goals
- Specify the level of authority the employee has in completing the task
- Encourage questions and provide all necessary resources

c) Grant Necessary Authority

Empower employees to make decisions related to the delegated task:

- Clearly define the scope of their decision-making power
- Avoid micromanaging; trust your employees to handle the responsibility
- Be available for guidance but allow space for independent problem-solving

d) Establish Check-ins

Regular progress updates ensure the task stays on track:

- Set up periodic check-ins, but avoid micromanaging

- Use these check-ins as opportunities for feedback and guidance
- Adjust the frequency of check-ins based on the employee's experience and the task complexity

e) Provide Feedback

Constructive feedback is crucial for employee development:

- Offer specific, actionable feedback on completed work
- Acknowledge successes and discuss areas for improvement
- Use feedback as a learning opportunity for future tasks

Task Prioritization and Management

Effective task management ensures that your team's efforts are focused on the most important work.

a) Use Prioritization Techniques

Implement structured prioritization methods:

- Eisenhower Matrix: Categorize tasks based on urgency and importance

- ABC Method: Assign high (A), medium (B), or low (C) priority to tasks
- MoSCoW Method: Categorize tasks as Must have, Should have, Could have, or Won't have

b) Implement Time Management Tools

Leverage technology to improve task management:

- Project management software (e.g., Trello, Asana, JIRA) for task tracking and collaboration
- Time tracking tools to understand how time is being spent
- Calendar management tools for scheduling and time blocking

c) Encourage Focus Time

Create an environment conducive to deep work:

- Implement "no meeting" blocks for focused work
- Encourage the use of techniques like the Pomodoro method (25 minutes of focused work followed by a 5-minute break)
- Create quiet spaces or allow work-from-home days for tasks requiring high concentration

d) Regular Team Check-ins

Maintain alignment and address issues promptly:

- Hold daily or weekly stand-ups to align priorities and discuss blockers
- Use these meetings to redistribute work if necessary
- Keep meetings focused and time-boxed to respect everyone's time

e) Workload Balancing

Ensure work is distributed fairly and effectively:

- Regularly review team workloads
- Be prepared to redistribute tasks if some team members are overloaded
- Consider skills, experience, and development goals when assigning tasks
- Use capacity planning tools to forecast resource needs and prevent burnout

Remember, effective human resource allocation is an ongoing process. Regularly review your team's performance, satisfaction, and development needs. Be prepared to adjust your strategies as your business grows and evolves.

By focusing on hiring the right people, investing in their development, and implementing effective delegation and task management practices, you can maximize the impact of your human resources. This not only drives productivity and innovation but also creates a positive work environment that attracts and retains top talent.

In the next chapter, we'll explore technological resource allocation, an increasingly important aspect of resource management in our digital age.

Chapter 6: Technological Resource Allocation

We all know that technology plays a crucial role in almost every aspect of business operations in our world today. Proper allocation of technological resources can significantly enhance productivity, streamline operations, and provide a competitive edge. This chapter will explore key aspects of technological resource allocation, providing in-depth guidance for small business owners and managers.

Choosing the Right Technology

Selecting the appropriate technology for your business is a critical decision that can have long-lasting impacts on your operations and bottom line. This section will delve into the process of evaluating your technological needs and making informed decisions about software and hardware investments.

Evaluating Software and Hardware Needs

a) Assess Current Systems

Before implementing new technology, it's crucial to thoroughly evaluate your existing systems:

- Conduct a comprehensive audit of your current technology infrastructure, including hardware, software, and network systems.
- Identify strengths and weaknesses of existing technology. What's working well? What's causing bottlenecks or inefficiencies?
- Determine what needs to be upgraded or replaced. Is your current technology outdated, slowing down operations, or causing security risks?
- Gather feedback from employees who use the systems daily. They often have valuable insights into pain points and potential improvements.
- Analyze your current technology costs, including maintenance, support, and any recurring licensing fees.

b) Define Requirements

Once you've assessed your current systems, the next step is to clearly define your requirements for new technology:

- List essential features and functionalities. What capabilities are absolutely necessary for your business operations?

- Consider future needs and scalability. Will the technology be able to grow with your business over the next 3-5 years?
- Identify any industry-specific requirements or compliance standards that the technology must meet.
- Prioritize your requirements. Distinguish between "must-have" and "nice-to-have" features.
- Consider the user experience. Will the technology be easy for your staff to learn and use effectively?
- Think about integration capabilities. How well will the new technology work with your existing systems?

c) Research Options

With your requirements in hand, it's time to explore the available options:

- Explore different vendors and solutions. Look beyond the market leaders to niche providers who might better suit your specific needs.
- Read reviews and case studies, particularly from businesses similar to yours in size and industry.

- Consider both off-the-shelf and custom solutions. While custom solutions can be tailored to your exact needs, they often come with higher costs and longer implementation times.
- Attend technology trade shows or webinars to learn about the latest innovations in your field.
- Consult with IT professionals or technology consultants for expert advice.
- Investigate open-source options, which can offer cost savings and flexibility, but may require more technical expertise to implement and maintain.
- Consider cloud-based versus on-premises solutions, weighing factors like cost, scalability, and control.

d) Test Before Committing

Before making a final decision, it's crucial to thoroughly test potential solutions:

- Request demos or trial periods for any software you're considering. Most vendors offer these for free.

- Involve end-users in the evaluation process. The people who will be using the technology daily should have a say in the decision.
- Set up a pilot project or proof of concept to test the technology in your actual business environment.
- Develop a set of test scenarios that reflect your typical use cases and evaluate how well the technology performs.
- Assess the quality of customer support during the trial period. How responsive and helpful is the vendor?
- Consider the training requirements. How steep is the learning curve for your staff?

Cost vs. Benefit of Technological Investments

When considering technological investments, it's crucial to weigh the costs against the potential benefits. This involves a comprehensive analysis that goes beyond just the initial purchase price.

a) Total Cost of Ownership (TCO)

The Total Cost of Ownership provides a more accurate picture of the true cost of technology over its lifetime:

- Initial purchase cost: This includes the upfront cost of hardware, software licenses, or subscription fees.
- Implementation costs: Consider expenses related to installation, configuration, and data migration.
- Training costs: Factor in the time and resources needed to train your staff on the new technology.
- Ongoing maintenance and support costs: This might include annual licensing fees, regular updates, and technical support.
- Upgrade costs: Consider how often you'll need to upgrade the technology and what those upgrades might cost.
- Infrastructure costs: You may need to upgrade your network or other systems to support the new technology.
- Operational costs: Factor in any changes to operational processes or staffing that might result from the new technology.

b) Return on Investment (ROI)

Calculating the potential ROI helps justify the investment and set expectations:

- Estimate potential savings: This could include reduced labor costs, lower error rates, or decreased downtime.
- Project revenue increases: Consider how the technology might help you serve more customers, enter new markets, or increase sales.
- Quantify productivity improvements: Estimate how much time could be saved or how many more tasks could be completed with the new technology.
- Consider intangible benefits: These might include improved customer satisfaction, better employee morale, or enhanced brand reputation.
- Use ROI calculation tools: Many vendors offer ROI calculators specific to their products. While these should be taken with a grain of salt, they can provide a starting point for your calculations.
- Consider the time frame for ROI: Some technologies may have a quick payback period, while others might take longer to show returns.

c) Implementation Costs

Implementation costs can sometimes be overlooked but can significantly impact the overall investment:

- Account for potential disruptions during implementation: Consider the cost of downtime or reduced productivity during the transition period.
- Include costs of data migration: Moving data from old systems to new ones can be time-consuming and complex.
- Factor in staff training: This includes both the direct costs of training programs and the indirect costs of reduced productivity while staff learn the new system.
- Consider customization costs: If you need the technology tailored to your specific needs, this can add significantly to the implementation costs.
- Plan for change management: There may be costs associated with managing the organizational changes that come with new technology.

d) Compatibility

Ensuring new technology integrates well with your existing systems is crucial:

- Evaluate integration requirements: Determine what systems the new technology needs to work with and how complex those integrations might be.
- Consider costs of any necessary customizations: If off-the-shelf integrations aren't available, you may need to budget for custom development.
- Assess the impact on existing workflows: How will the new technology affect your current processes? Will it require significant changes to how your team works?
- Plan for data synchronization: If you'll be running multiple systems in parallel, consider the costs and complexity of keeping data synchronized.
- Evaluate long-term compatibility: Will the new technology continue to work with your other systems as they evolve over time?

Remember, the cheapest option isn't always the most cost-effective in the long run. Consider the long-term value and potential for scalability when making technology decisions. A more expensive solution that integrates well with your existing systems, offers robust support, and can grow with your business may provide better value over time than a cheaper alternative that falls short in these areas.

Automation and Efficiency

Automation can significantly improve efficiency and free up human resources for more strategic tasks. This section explores how to identify opportunities for automation and implement it effectively in your business.

Implementing Automation Tools

a) Identify Repetitive Tasks

The first step in implementing automation is to identify tasks that are good candidates for automation:

- Look for processes that are time-consuming and prone to human error. These are often the best candidates for automation.
- Conduct a thorough process analysis across all departments. You might find automation opportunities in unexpected places.
- Focus on high-volume, rules-based tasks. These typically offer the biggest returns on automation investments.

- Consider both customer-facing and internal processes for automation.
- Look for tasks that require data to be inputted multiple times across different systems. These are often ripe for automation.
- Identify bottlenecks in your workflows where automation could speed things up.

b) Choose Appropriate Tools

Once you've identified tasks to automate, the next step is selecting the right tools:

- Customer Relationship Management (CRM): Automate customer data management, sales processes, and marketing campaigns.
- Examples: Salesforce, HubSpot, Zoho CRM
- Benefits: Improved customer tracking, more effective sales processes, better marketing ROI
- Marketing automation: Streamline email marketing, social media posting, and lead nurturing.
- Examples: Mailchimp, Marketo, HubSpot Marketing

- Benefits: More consistent customer communication, improved lead scoring, better campaign tracking
- Inventory management: Automate stock level tracking, reordering, and forecasting.
- Examples: TradeGecko, Cin7, Fishbowl
- Benefits: Reduced stockouts, lower carrying costs, improved cash flow
- Accounting and invoicing: Automate bookkeeping tasks, invoice generation, and payment tracking.
- Examples: QuickBooks, Xero, FreshBooks
- Benefits: Faster invoice processing, fewer errors, better financial reporting
- Project management: Automate task assignments, progress tracking, and team communication.
- Examples: Asana, Trello, Microsoft Project
- Benefits: Improved team coordination, better resource allocation, more accurate project timelines
- Human Resources: Automate payroll processing, time tracking, and benefits administration.
- Examples: BambooHR, Gusto, ADP

- Benefits: Reduced administrative overhead, improved compliance, better employee experience

When choosing tools, consider factors like:

- Ease of use
- Integration capabilities with your existing systems
- Scalability as your business grows
- Cost (both upfront and ongoing)
- Available support and training resources

c) Start Small

When implementing automation, it's often best to start small and scale up:

- Begin with one or two processes: Choose processes that are relatively simple and have a clear potential for improvement through automation.
- Run pilot programs: Test automation solutions in a limited context before rolling them out company-wide.
- Measure results: Establish clear metrics to evaluate the success of your automation efforts.

This might include time saved, error rates reduced, or costs decreased.

- Gather feedback: Collect input from employees using the automated systems. Their insights can help you refine and improve your automation strategy.
- Iterate and improve: Use the lessons learned from your initial automation efforts to inform and improve future implementations.
- Gradually expand automation: As you see benefits and gain experience, expand your automation efforts to more complex processes or additional areas of the business.

d) Train Staff

Proper training is crucial for the successful implementation of automation tools:

- Ensure employees understand how to use new tools: Provide comprehensive training on all aspects of the automated systems.
- Emphasize the benefits of automation: Help employees understand how automation will make their jobs easier or more interesting, not replace them.

- Provide ongoing support: Offer resources for employees to get help when they encounter issues or have questions.
- Create user guides and documentation: Develop easy-to-follow guides that employees can reference as needed.
- Designate power users: Identify employees who quickly grasp the new systems and can serve as resources for their colleagues.
- Address concerns: Be open to feedback and address any concerns employees might have about the automation process.
- Celebrate successes: Recognize and reward employees who effectively leverage automation to improve their work.

Streamlining Operations with Technology

Beyond automation, there are many ways technology can help streamline your business operations:

a) Process Mapping

Before implementing new technology, it's crucial to understand your current processes:

- Document current processes: Create detailed flowcharts or diagrams of how work currently flows through your organization.
- Identify bottlenecks and inefficiencies: Look for areas where work frequently gets held up or where errors often occur.
- Involve employees in the mapping process: Those closest to the work often have the best insights into how processes could be improved.
- Use process mapping software: Tools like Lucidchart or Microsoft Visio can help create clear, easy-to-understand process maps.
- Analyze value stream: Identify which steps in your processes add value and which don't. Look to eliminate or minimize non-value-adding steps.
- Consider customer perspective: Map out the customer journey to identify areas where technology could improve the customer experience.

b) Integration

Integrating different systems can significantly improve efficiency:

- Look for opportunities to integrate different systems: Identify where data is being manually transferred between systems.
- Reduce manual data entry and duplicate efforts: Automated data transfer between systems can save time and reduce errors.
- Consider middleware solutions: These can help connect disparate systems that don't have built-in integration capabilities.
- Implement API-driven architecture: This can make it easier to connect different software systems and share data.
- Evaluate Enterprise Resource Planning (ERP) systems: For larger or growing businesses, an ERP system can provide comprehensive integration across all business processes.
- Prioritize integration efforts: Focus first on integrating systems that handle your most critical or high-volume processes.

c) Cloud Solutions

Cloud-based tools can offer improved accessibility and collaboration:

- Consider cloud-based alternatives to on-premises software: These often offer greater flexibility and scalability.
- Evaluate Software-as-a-Service (SaaS) options: These can reduce IT overhead and provide automatic updates and maintenance.
- Implement cloud storage solutions: Tools like Dropbox or Google Drive can improve file sharing and collaboration.
- Use cloud-based productivity suites: Solutions like Google Workspace or Microsoft 365 can enhance team collaboration and communication.
- Consider hybrid cloud solutions: These can offer a balance between the flexibility of the cloud and the control of on-premises systems.
- Assess security measures: Ensure any cloud solutions you adopt have robust security measures in place to protect your data.

d) Mobile Technology

Implementing mobile solutions can improve flexibility and responsiveness:

- Develop mobile-friendly versions of key business applications: This allows employees to work effectively from anywhere.
- Implement Mobile Device Management (MDM) solutions: These help secure and manage company data on employee devices.
- Consider BYOD (Bring Your Own Device) policies: This can reduce hardware costs but requires careful management of security risks.
- Use mobile apps for field service or sales teams: This can improve efficiency for employees who work outside the office.
- Implement mobile payment solutions: For retail or service businesses, this can improve the customer experience and speed up transactions.
- Leverage location-based services: These can be useful for logistics, delivery services, or location-based marketing.

e) Data Analytics

Using data analysis tools can provide valuable insights to inform decision-making:

- Implement Business Intelligence (BI) tools: Solutions like Tableau or Power BI can help visualize and analyze business data.
- Use predictive analytics: This can help forecast trends, customer behavior, or potential issues before they occur.
- Implement real-time analytics: This allows for immediate insights and faster decision-making.
- Consider big data solutions: For businesses dealing with large volumes of data, big data tools can uncover hidden patterns and correlations.
- Use A/B testing tools: These can help optimize websites, marketing campaigns, and product features.
- Implement customer analytics: Tools that analyze customer behavior can help improve marketing efforts and customer service.
- Use operational analytics: These can help identify inefficiencies in business processes and opportunities for improvement.

Cybersecurity Considerations

As businesses become more reliant on technology, cybersecurity becomes increasingly important. This section explores key considerations and best practices for protecting your digital assets.

Protecting Digital Resources

a) Regular Updates

Keeping your systems up-to-date is one of the most important steps in maintaining cybersecurity:

- Keep all software and systems up-to-date: This includes operating systems, applications, and firmware on network devices.
- Apply security patches promptly: Many cyberattacks exploit known vulnerabilities that have already been patched.
- Implement an automated update system: This ensures updates are applied consistently across all systems.
- Test updates before wide deployment: This can help catch any compatibility issues before they affect your whole organization.
- Have a rollback plan: In case an update causes unexpected issues, have a plan to revert to the previous stable version.

- Keep an inventory of all software and systems: This helps ensure nothing is overlooked in the update process.

b) Strong Access Controls

Implementing robust access controls is crucial for protecting your digital resources:

- Implement strong password policies: Require complex passwords and regular password changes.
- Use multi-factor authentication (MFA) where possible: This adds an extra layer of security beyond just passwords.
- Implement the principle of least privilege: Give users only the access rights they need to do their jobs.
- Regularly review and update access rights: Remove access for employees who have left or changed roles.
- Use Single Sign-On (SSO) solutions: This can improve security and user experience for accessing multiple systems.
- Implement account lockout policies: This helps prevent brute force attacks on user accounts.

- Use biometric authentication where appropriate: This can provide an additional layer of security for sensitive systems.

c) Data Encryption

Encrypting sensitive data protects it even if unauthorized access occurs:

- Encrypt sensitive data, both in transit and at rest: This includes customer data, financial information, and proprietary business data.
- Use strong encryption protocols: Stay up-to-date with the latest encryption standards.
- Implement full-disk encryption on all devices: This protects data if a device is lost or stolen.
- Use encrypted communication channels: Implement VPNs for remote access and use encrypted email for sensitive communications.
- Manage encryption keys securely: Establish processes for securely storing and rotating encryption keys.
- Train employees on the importance of encryption: Ensure they understand when and how to use encrypted communications.

d) Regular Backups

A robust backup strategy is crucial for recovering from cyber incidents:

- Implement a regular backup schedule: The frequency should be based on how often your data changes and how much data loss your business can tolerate.
- Follow the 3-2-1 backup rule: Keep at least three copies of your data, on two different types of storage media, with one copy stored off-site.
- Test data recovery processes regularly: Ensure you can actually restore from your backups when needed.
- Encrypt backup data: This protects your backups from unauthorized access.
- Implement version control: Keep multiple versions of backups to protect against ransomware that might encrypt your most recent backup.
- Automate the backup process: This reduces the risk of human error and ensures consistency.
- Store backups securely: Ensure physical security for on-site backups and use reputable cloud providers for off-site storage.

e) Employee Training

Your employees are often your first line of defense against cyber threats:

- Educate staff about cybersecurity best practices: Cover topics like password security, phishing awareness, and safe internet usage.
- Conduct regular security awareness training: Cyber threats evolve rapidly, so ongoing education is crucial.
- Use simulated phishing attacks: These can help employees recognize and respond to real phishing attempts.
- Provide clear guidelines for handling sensitive data: Ensure employees understand their responsibilities in protecting company information.
- Encourage a culture of security: Make it easy for employees to report suspicious activities or potential security breaches.
- Tailor training to different roles: Employees in different positions may face different types of cyber risks.
- Measure the effectiveness of training: Use metrics like reduced click rates on phishing simulations to gauge improvement over time.

Best Practices for Small Businesses

Small businesses often have limited resources for cybersecurity, but there are several cost-effective measures they can implement:

a) Use a Firewall

Firewalls are a crucial first line of defense for your network:

- Implement both hardware and software firewalls: This provides multiple layers of protection.
- Configure firewalls properly: Ensure they're set up to block unnecessary incoming and outgoing traffic.
- Regularly update firewall rules: Review and adjust rules as your network needs change.
- Use Next-Generation Firewalls (NGFW): These provide more advanced features like intrusion prevention and application-level filtering.
- Enable logging: This can help you detect and investigate potential security incidents.

b) Secure Wi-Fi Networks

Unsecured Wi-Fi can be an easy entry point for cybercriminals:

- Use strong encryption (WPA3): This is the latest and most secure Wi-Fi encryption standard.
- Change default passwords on network devices: Default passwords are often well-known and easily guessed.
- Hide your network SSID: While not foolproof, this can make your network less visible to casual attackers.
- Use a guest network: This keeps visitors separate from your main business network.
- Regularly update router firmware: This ensures you have the latest security patches.
- Use a VPN for remote access: This encrypts connections from off-site locations.

c) Limit Access

Restricting access to sensitive data can limit the potential damage from a breach:

- Provide employees access only to the data they need: This follows the principle of least privilege.

- Use role-based access control (RBAC): This makes it easier to manage access rights as employees change roles.
- Implement network segmentation: This can contain the spread of malware or limit the reach of an attacker.
- Use strong authentication for admin accounts: These high-privilege accounts should have extra protection.
- Regularly audit user access: Review who has access to what data and revoke unnecessary permissions.
- Implement time-based access controls: Limit access to sensitive systems to business hours when possible.

d) Use Antivirus Software

Antivirus software is a basic but crucial component of cybersecurity:

- Install reputable antivirus software on all devices: This includes computers, servers, and mobile devices.

- Keep it updated: Ensure antivirus definitions are updated regularly to protect against the latest threats.
- Run regular scans: Schedule automatic scans to catch any threats that might have slipped through.
- Consider endpoint detection and response (EDR) solutions: These provide more advanced threat detection and response capabilities.
- Educate employees on the importance of not disabling antivirus software: Sometimes employees turn it off if they think it's slowing down their computer.

e) Have a Response Plan

Being prepared for a cyber incident can significantly reduce its impact:

- Develop an incident response plan: This should outline steps to take in case of different types of cyber incidents.
- Assign roles and responsibilities: Ensure everyone knows their part in responding to an incident.

- Know who to contact: Have a list of key contacts, including IT support, legal counsel, and law enforcement.
- Practice your response: Conduct tabletop exercises to test your plan and identify areas for improvement.
- Have a communication strategy: Plan how you'll communicate with employees, customers, and the public if needed.
- Document everything: Keep detailed records of any incidents and your response for future reference and potential legal needs.

f) Consider Cyber Insurance

Cyber insurance can provide a financial safety net in case of a cyber incident:

- Evaluate the need for cyber liability insurance: This can help cover costs associated with data breaches or other cyber incidents.
- Understand what's covered: Policies can vary widely, so make sure you know exactly what protection you're getting.

- Consider first-party and third-party coverage: First-party covers your direct losses, while third-party covers your liability to others.
- Look for policies that include incident response services: Some policies provide access to cybersecurity experts to help you respond to an incident.
- Review coverage limits: Ensure they're adequate for your potential risks.
- Understand your obligations: Many policies require you to maintain certain security measures to be eligible for coverage.

Remember, cybersecurity is not a one-time task but an ongoing process. Regularly review and update your security measures to protect against evolving threats. Stay informed about new types of cyber threats and adjust your defenses accordingly.

Chapter 6 Summary

By carefully choosing the right technology, leveraging automation for efficiency, and prioritizing cybersecurity, you can make the most of your technological resources. This not only improves your operations but also protects your business from potential threats.

Effective technological resource allocation requires a strategic approach. It involves understanding your business needs, carefully evaluating options, considering long-term costs and benefits, and implementing solutions in a way that minimizes disruption and maximizes adoption.

Remember that technology is a tool to support your business goals, not an end in itself. Always tie your technology decisions back to your overall business strategy and objectives. Be prepared to adapt as technology and your business needs evolve.

Finally, don't underestimate the importance of your people in making technology work for your business. Invest in training, encourage feedback, and foster a culture that embraces technological change while maintaining a focus on your core business values and objectives.

In the next chapter, we'll explore physical and operational resource allocation, focusing on how to optimize your tangible assets and operational processes. This will complement the technological resources discussed in this chapter, providing a comprehensive approach to resource management for your small business.

Chapter 7: Physical and Operational Resource Allocation

Physical and operational resources form the backbone of many businesses, especially those in manufacturing, retail, or service industries. Effective allocation of these resources can significantly impact your productivity, customer satisfaction, and bottom line. Let's explore key aspects of physical and operational resource allocation.

Optimizing Physical Assets

Physical assets include everything from your inventory to your equipment and facilities. Here's how to make the most of these resources:

Managing Inventory

a) Implement Inventory Management Systems:

- Use software to track stock levels in real-time
- Set up automatic reorder points

b) Just-in-Time (JIT) Inventory:

- Minimize inventory holding costs

- Ensure you have what you need when you need it

c) ABC Analysis:

- Categorize inventory based on importance and value
- Focus more attention on high-value items

d) Regular Audits:

- Conduct physical inventory counts regularly
- Reconcile with system records

Maintenance of Equipment and Facilities

a) Preventive Maintenance:

- Schedule regular maintenance to prevent breakdowns
- Keep detailed maintenance logs

b) Predictive Maintenance:

- Use data and analytics to predict when maintenance will be needed
- Minimize unexpected downtime

c) Equipment Upgrades:

- Regularly assess if equipment needs to be replaced or upgraded
- Consider energy efficiency and technological advancements

d) Facility Management:

- Optimize space utilization
- Ensure a safe and productive work environment

Operational Efficiency

Improving operational efficiency is about doing more with less, without compromising on quality. Here are some strategies:

Lean Management Principles

a) Value Stream Mapping:

- Identify and eliminate non-value-adding activities

b) Continuous Improvement (Kaizen):

- Encourage all employees to suggest improvements
- Implement small, incremental changes regularly

c) 5S Methodology:

- Sort, Set in order, Shine, Standardize, Sustain
- Create an organized and efficient workplace

d) Pull Systems:

- Produce based on actual demand rather than forecasts

Reducing Waste and Increasing Productivity

a) Identify and Eliminate Bottlenecks:

- Use process mapping to identify constraints
- Allocate resources to alleviate bottlenecks

b) Standardize Processes:

- Create standard operating procedures (SOPs)
- Ensure consistency and efficiency

c) Cross-Training:

- Train employees in multiple roles
- Increase flexibility and reduce dependence on individuals

d) Leverage Technology:

- Use automation where appropriate
- Implement productivity-enhancing software

Sustainability and Green Practices

Incorporating sustainability into your resource allocation not only benefits the environment but can also lead to cost savings and improved brand image.

Environmental Considerations

a) Energy Efficiency:

- Upgrade to energy-efficient lighting and equipment
- Implement smart building systems

b) Waste Reduction:

- Implement recycling programs
- Look for ways to reduce packaging

c) Sustainable Sourcing:

- Choose suppliers with sustainable practices
- Consider local sourcing to reduce transportation emissions

d) Water Conservation:

- Install water-efficient fixtures
- Implement rainwater harvesting systems where feasible
- Regularly check for and fix leaks

Implementing Green Practices

a) Green Office Policies:

- Encourage paperless operations
- Promote energy-saving habits among employees

b) Sustainable Transportation:

- Offer incentives for carpooling or using public transport
- Consider electric or hybrid vehicles for company use

c) Green Building Design:

- Use sustainable materials in construction or renovation
- Implement green roofs or solar panels where possible

d) Measure and Report:

- Track your environmental impact
- Set sustainability goals and report progress

Remember, sustainability isn't just about being environmentally friendly. It's also about creating long-term value and resilience for your business.

Supply Chain Optimization

For many businesses, especially those in manufacturing or retail, effective supply chain management is crucial for operational efficiency.

Supplier Management

a) Supplier Evaluation:

- Regularly assess suppliers based on quality, cost, and reliability
- Develop strong relationships with key suppliers

b) Diversification:

- Avoid over-reliance on a single supplier
- Have backup suppliers for critical components

c) Collaboration:

- Work closely with suppliers to improve processes
- Share forecasts to help suppliers plan better

Logistics Optimization

a) Route Planning:

- Use software to optimize delivery routes
- Consider consolidating shipments

b) Warehouse Management:

- Optimize warehouse layout for efficiency
- Use warehouse management systems for better tracking

c) Last-Mile Delivery:

- Consider partnering with local delivery services
- Explore innovative options like click-and-collect

d) Reverse Logistics:

- Have an efficient system for handling returns
- Consider how to reuse or recycle returned items

Capacity Planning

Effective capacity planning ensures that you have the right resources available at the right time to meet demand.

Forecasting Demand

a) Use Historical Data:

- Analyze past sales trends
- Consider seasonal fluctuations

b) Market Analysis:

- Keep an eye on market trends and competitor actions
- Consider economic factors that might impact demand

c) Collaborative Planning:

- Work with sales and marketing teams for more accurate forecasts

Managing Capacity

a) Flexible Capacity:

- Use temporary workers or overtime to handle peak periods

- Consider outsourcing non-core activities

b) Equipment Utilization:

- Maximize the use of existing equipment
- Consider shift work to increase production hours

c) Balancing Act:

- Strive for a balance between having enough capacity to meet demand and avoiding excess capacity

d) Regular Review:

- Continuously monitor capacity utilization
- Adjust plans as needed based on actual demand

By optimizing your physical assets, improving operational efficiency, implementing sustainable practices, optimizing your supply chain, and effective capacity planning, you can make the most of your physical and operational resources. This not only improves your bottom line but also enhances your ability to meet customer needs and adapt to changing market conditions.

In the next chapter, we'll explore how to integrate these various aspects of resource allocation into a cohesive strategy, and how to continuously monitor and adjust your resource allocation for optimal business performance.

Chapter 8: Integrating and Optimizing Resource Allocation

Now that we've explored the key areas of resource allocation - financial, human, technological, and physical/operational - it's time to look at how to bring these elements together into a cohesive strategy. Effective resource allocation isn't about optimizing each area in isolation, but rather about finding the right balance that best supports your overall business goals.

Creating a Holistic Resource Allocation Strategy

Align with Business Goals:

1. **Review Your Business Strategy:**
   Ensure your resource allocation supports your long-term vision
   Identify key strategic initiatives that require resources

2. **Set Clear Priorities:**
   Rank initiatives based on their strategic importance
   Allocate resources accordingly

Cross-Functional Integration:

1. **Break Down Silos:**
   Encourage communication between different departments
   Create cross-functional teams for key projects
2. **Shared Resources:**
   Identify resources that can be shared across departments
   Implement systems for efficient resource sharing

Balance Short-Term and Long-Term Needs:

1. **Operational Efficiency:**
   Allocate resources to maintain day-to-day operations
2. **Strategic Investments:**
   Set aside resources for long-term growth initiatives
   Consider the balance between current operations and future potential

Risk Management:

1. **Identify Potential Risks:**
   Consider risks in each area of resource allocation
   Assess their potential impact on your business

2. **Mitigation Strategies:**
   Develop contingency plans
   Maintain some flexibility in your resource allocation

Implementing Resource Allocation Tools and Techniques

Resource Planning Software:

1. **Enterprise Resource Planning (ERP) Systems:**
   Integrate various business processes
   Provide real-time data for decision making

2. **Project Management Tools:**
   Allocate resources across different projects
   Track resource utilization and project progress

Data Analytics:

1. **Business Intelligence Tools:**
   Analyze data from various sources
   Generate insights to inform resource allocation decisions
2. **Predictive Analytics:**
   Use historical data to forecast future resource needs
   Identify potential bottlenecks or inefficiencies

Agile Methodologies:

1. **Iterative Approach:**
   Break down large initiatives into smaller, manageable chunks
   Allow for more flexible resource allocation
2. **Regular Review and Adjustment:**
   Conduct sprint reviews and retrospectives
   Quickly reallocate resources based on changing priorities

Continuous Monitoring and Optimization

Resource allocation isn't a one-time task, but an ongoing process of monitoring, evaluating, and adjusting.

Key Performance Indicators (KPIs):Key Performance Indicators (KPIs):

1. Define Relevant KPIs:
Financial metrics (ROI, profit margins)
Operational metrics (productivity, efficiency)
Customer-focused metrics (satisfaction, retention)

2. Regular Reporting:
Create dashboards for easy monitoring
Conduct regular review meetings

Feedback Loops:

1. Employee Feedback:
Regularly solicit input from those using the resources
Encourage suggestions for improvement

2. Customer Feedback:
Monitor customer satisfaction and complaints
Use feedback to inform resource allocation decisions

Market Monitoring:

1. **Competitor Analysis:**

   Keep an eye on how competitors are allocating resources

   Identify areas where you may need to increase investment

2. **Industry Trends:**

   Stay informed about emerging technologies or practices

   Be prepared to reallocate resources to stay competitive

Regular Audits:

1. **Internal Audits:**

   Conduct periodic reviews of resource utilization

   Identify areas of waste or inefficiency

2. **External Audits:**

   Consider bringing in outside experts for an objective view

   Use insights to refine your resource allocation strategy

Continuous Improvement:

1. **Learn from Experience:**

   Document lessons learned from past resource

allocation decisions

Apply these lessons to future planning

2. **Encourage Innovation:**

Allocate some resources to experimentation and innovation

Be willing to take calculated risks on new approaches

By integrating these elements into a cohesive strategy and continuously monitoring and optimizing your approach, you can ensure that your resource allocation remains effective and aligned with your business goals, even as your business and the market evolve.

Remember, effective resource allocation is not about having the most resources, but about making the most of the resources you have. It's about finding the right balance that allows your business to operate efficiently today while also investing in future growth and adaptability.

In our final chapter, we'll look at some case studies of successful resource allocation in action, and provide some final tips for implementing these strategies in your own business.

Chapter 9: Case Studies and Implementation Strategies

To bring our discussion of resource allocation to life, let's examine some real-world examples of effective resource allocation and discuss strategies for implementing these principles in your own business.

Case Studies

1. **Tech Startup**: Agile Resource Allocation
   Company: A small software development startup
   Challenge: Limited resources, rapidly changing market demands Solution:
   - Implemented Agile methodologies for project management
   - Used cloud-based tools for flexible resource allocation
   - Emphasized cross-training to create a versatile workforce
   - Regularly reprioritized projects based on market feedback

   Result: The company was able to pivot quickly, launching successful products despite limited resources. Employee satisfaction improved due to varied work and clear goals.

2. **Manufacturing Company:** Lean Principles
Company: A medium-sized furniture manufacturer
Challenge: Inefficient processes, high inventory costs Solution:
   - Applied Lean manufacturing principles
   - Implemented Just-in-Time inventory management
   - Invested in employee training for continuous improvement
   - Used data analytics to optimize production scheduling

Result: Reduced inventory costs by 30%, improved production efficiency by 25%, and increased employee engagement in process improvement.

3. **Retail Chain**: Omnichannel Resource Allocation
Company: A national clothing retailer
Challenge: Balancing resources between physical stores and e-commerce Solution:

- Implemented an integrated inventory management system
- Trained store staff to handle online order fulfillment
- Used predictive analytics for demand forecasting
- Reallocated marketing budget towards digital channels

Result: Achieved a 40% increase in online sales without significantly impacting in-store performance. Improved overall inventory turnover and customer satisfaction.

4. **Service Company**: Human Resource Optimization
Company: A growing IT consulting firm
Challenge: High employee turnover, difficulty matching skills to projects Solution:
- Implemented a comprehensive skills database
- Developed a career progression framework
- Used project management software for resource allocation

- Invested in continuous learning and development programs

Result: Reduced employee turnover by 50%, improved project delivery times, and increased customer satisfaction scores.

Implementation Strategies

Now, let's discuss how you can implement effective resource allocation strategies in your own business:

1. **Start with a Comprehensive Assessment:**
   - Audit your current resources across all categories
   - Identify areas of waste or inefficiency
   - Assess how well your current allocation aligns with business goals
2. **Develop a Clear Resource Allocation Plan:**
   - Set specific, measurable goals for resource utilization
   - Prioritize initiatives based on strategic importance
   - Create a timeline for implementation
3. **Invest in the Right Tools:**
   - Choose software that fits your business needs and scale

- Ensure tools can integrate with your existing systems
- Provide thorough training to ensure adoption

4. **Foster a Culture of Efficiency:**
   - Communicate the importance of effective resource use
   - Encourage employees to suggest improvements
   - Recognize and reward efficient resource use

5. **Implement Gradually:**
   - Start with pilot projects or single departments
   - Learn from initial implementation before scaling up
   - Be prepared to adjust your approach based on feedback

6. **Continuously Monitor and Adjust:**
   - Regularly review KPIs related to resource utilization
   - Conduct periodic audits of resource allocation
   - Stay flexible and be willing to reallocate resources as needed

7. **Emphasize Training and Development:**
    - Invest in training employees on new systems and processes
    - Develop skills that allow for more flexible resource allocation
    - Encourage cross-functional knowledge sharing
8. **Balance Short-Term and Long-Term Needs:**
    - Allocate resources to maintain current operations
    - Set aside resources for strategic initiatives and innovation
    - Regularly reassess the balance based on business performance and market conditions
9. **Embrace Technology:**
    - Use data analytics for informed decision-making
    - Consider automation for repetitive tasks
    - Stay informed about emerging technologies in your industry
10. **Seek External Input:**
    - Consider bringing in consultants for specialized expertise

- o Benchmark your resource allocation against industry standards
- o Network with peers to share best practices

Remember, effective resource allocation is an ongoing process, not a one-time event. It requires continuous attention, analysis, and adjustment. However, by implementing these strategies and learning from successful examples, you can significantly improve your business's efficiency, adaptability, and overall performance.

As you move forward with implementing these resource allocation strategies, keep in mind that every business is unique. What works for one company may not work exactly the same way for another. Be prepared to adapt these principles to fit your specific situation, industry, and business goals.

With careful planning, consistent effort, and a willingness to learn and adjust, you can master the art of resource allocation and position your business for long-term success.

Overcoming Common Challenges in Resource Allocation

As you implement your resource allocation strategy, you're likely to encounter some common challenges. Here's how to address them:

1. **Resistance to Change:**
   - Communicate the benefits of new allocation strategies clearly
   - Involve employees in the planning process
   - Provide ample training and support during transitions
2. **Data Overload:**
   - Focus on key metrics that align with your business goals
   - Use data visualization tools to make information more digestible
   - Invest in data analysis skills within your team
3. **Balancing Flexibility and Consistency:**
   - Establish clear guidelines for resource allocation
   - Build in regular review periods to allow for adjustments
   - Create contingency plans for unexpected changes

4. **Managing Competing Priorities:**
   - Develop a clear prioritization framework
   - Encourage open communication between departments
   - Use objective criteria for decision-making
5. **Dealing with Resource Constraints:**
   - Focus on efficiency and optimization
   - Consider alternative resource models (e.g., outsourcing, partnerships)
   - Be creative in finding low-cost solutions

Future Trends in Resource Allocation

As we look to the future, several trends are likely to impact how businesses allocate their resources:

1. **Artificial Intelligence and Machine Learning:**
   - AI-driven predictive analytics for more accurate forecasting
   - Automated resource allocation based on real-time data
   - Machine learning algorithms for optimizing complex allocation decisions
2. **Increased Focus on Sustainability:**

- Greater emphasis on sustainable resource use
- Integration of environmental impact into allocation decisions
- New metrics for measuring resource efficiency

3. **Gig Economy and Flexible Workforce:**
   - More dynamic allocation of human resources
   - Increased use of freelancers and contract workers
   - New tools for managing distributed teams

4. **Internet of Things (IoT):**
   - Real-time tracking of physical assets
   - Predictive maintenance to optimize equipment use
   - More granular data for resource allocation decisions

5. **Blockchain Technology:**
   - Improved supply chain transparency
   - More efficient resource tracking and allocation
   - New models for resource sharing across organizations

Conclusion

Effective resource allocation is a critical skill for any business leader. It's about making the most of what you have, aligning your resources with your strategic goals, and continuously adapting to changing circumstances.

Throughout this guide, we've explored the key principles of resource allocation across various categories - financial, human, technological, and physical/operational. We've discussed strategies for creating a holistic approach, implementing the right tools and techniques, and continuously monitoring and optimizing your allocation.

Remember, there's no one-size-fits-all solution to resource allocation. The best approach for your business will depend on your specific circumstances, industry, and goals. However, by applying the principles and strategies we've discussed, you can create a more efficient, adaptable, and successful organization.

As you move forward, keep these key takeaways in mind:

1. Align your resource allocation with your strategic goals
2. Maintain flexibility to adapt to changing circumstances
3. Use data to inform your decisions, but don't neglect human insight
4. Encourage a culture of efficiency and continuous improvement
5. Regularly review and adjust your allocation strategy
6. Invest in the right tools and technologies to support your efforts
7. Balance short-term needs with long-term investments
8. Consider the interdependencies between different types of resources
9. Stay informed about industry trends and best practices
10. Remember that effective resource allocation is an ongoing process, not a one-time task

By mastering the art of resource allocation, you'll be well-positioned to navigate the challenges of today's business environment and seize the opportunities of tomorrow. Good luck on your journey to more effective resource management!.

Appendices

A. Templates and Worksheets

1. Budget Template:

```
1    Annual Budget Template
2
3    Income:
4       - Revenue Stream 1:      $_____
5       - Revenue Stream 2:      $_____
6       - Revenue Stream 3:      $_____
7    Total Income:               $_____
8
9    Expenses:
10      Fixed Costs:
11         - Rent:               $_____
12         - Salaries:           $_____
13         - Insurance:          $_____
14      Variable Costs:
15         - Materials:          $_____
16         - Marketing:          $_____
17         - Utilities:          $_____
18   Total Expenses:             $_____
19
20   Net Profit/Loss:            $_____
```

2. SWOT Analysis Worksheet:

2. SWOT Analysis Worksheet:

```
 1 │ SWOT Analysis
 2 │
 3 │ Strengths:
 4 │ 1. _____
 5 │ 2. _____
 6 │ 3. _____
 7 │
 8 │ Weaknesses:
 9 │ 1. _____
10 │ 2. _____
11 │ 3. _____
12 │
13 │ Opportunities:
14 │ 1. _____
15 │ 2. _____
16 │ 3. _____
17 │
18 │ Threats:
19 │ 1. _____
20 │ 2. _____
21 │ 3. _____
22 │
23 │ Action Items:
24 │ 1. _____
25 │ 2. _____
26 │ 3. _____
```

3. Time Management Sheet:

3. Time Management Sheet:

```
Daily Time Management Sheet

Date: ___/___/____

Time          Activity              Priority (H/M/L)   Completed
8:00 AM     _____      _____      [ ]
9:00 AM     _____      _____      [ ]
10:00 AM    _____      _____      [ ]
11:00 AM    _____      _____      [ ]
12:00 PM    _____      _____      [ ]
1:00 PM     _____      _____      [ ]
2:00 PM     _____      _____      [ ]
3:00 PM     _____      _____      [ ]
4:00 PM     _____      _____      [ ]
5:00 PM     _____      _____      [ ]

Reflections:
_____
_____
```

B. Resource List

Books:

1. "Good to Great" by Jim Collins
2. "The Lean Startup" by Eric Ries
3. "Scaling Up" by Verne Harnish
4. "The Effective Executive" by Peter Drucker
5. "Measure What Matters" by John Doerr

Websites:

1. Harvard Business Review (hbr.org)

2. MIT Sloan Management Review (sloanreview.mit.edu)
3. Project Management Institute (pmi.org)
4. Society for Human Resource Management (shrm.org)
5. TechCrunch (techcrunch.com)

Tools:

1. Asana (project management)
2. Trello (task management)
3. QuickBooks (financial management)
4. Salesforce (customer relationship management)
5. Tableau (data visualization)

C. References

1. Kaplan, R. S., & Norton, D. P. (1996). The balanced scorecard: translating strategy into action. Harvard Business Press.
2. Porter, M. E. (2008). The five competitive forces that shape strategy. Harvard Business Review, 86(1), 78-93.
3. Christensen, C. M. (2013). The innovator's dilemma: when new technologies cause great firms to fail. Harvard Business Review Press.

4. Osterwalder, A., & Pigneur, Y. (2010). Business model generation: a handbook for visionaries, game changers, and challengers. John Wiley & Sons.

5. Duhigg, C. (2012). The power of habit: Why we do what we do in life and business. Random House.

6. Ries, E. (2011). The lean startup: How today's entrepreneurs use continuous innovation to create radically successful businesses. Crown Business.

7. Sinek, S. (2009). Start with why: How great leaders inspire everyone to take action. Penguin.

8. Collins, J. C. (2001). Good to great: Why some companies make the leap... and others don't. Harper Business.

9. Kim, W. C., & Mauborgne, R. (2005). Blue ocean strategy: How to create uncontested market space and make the competition irrelevant. Harvard Business School Press.

10. Drucker, P. F. (2006). The effective executive: The definitive guide to getting the right things done. Harper Business.

These appendices provide practical tools for implementing the strategies discussed in the book, as well as resources for further learning and references to support the content. Readers can use these templates and worksheets to apply the concepts to their own businesses, explore additional resources to deepen their understanding, and verify the sources of information presented in the book.

ABOUT THE AUTHOR

Harrell Howard is a prolific author and thought leader, specializing in a diverse array of subjects that cater to both personal and professional development. With a deep passion for empowering readers through knowledge, Harrell has penned numerous best-selling books, each offering practical insights and actionable strategies across various fields.

Harrell Howard combines a rich background in technology, marketing, and personal development to deliver content that is both insightful and practical.

When he's not writing, Harrell enjoys exploring new tech, market trends, and sharing his knowledge via speaking engagements and workshops. His drive for lifelong learning & passion for helping others is evident in his book.

www.ingramcontent.com/pod-product-compliance
Lightning Source LLC
Chambersburg PA
CBHW071920210526
45479CB00002B/495